◆ THEORY AND PRACTICE ◆

The Struggling Reader

Interventions That Work

J. DAVID COOPER • DAVID J. CHARD • NANCY D. KIGER

NEW YORK • TORONTO • LONDON • AUCKLAND • SYDNEY
MEXICO CITY • NEW DELHI • HONG KONG • BUENOS AIRES

◆------ Dedications ------◆

To Michael, Melissa, David, Molly, and Cooper, the most important
people in my life, and to the memory of my mother, Isabelle. —JDC

To my first teachers, Mom, Dad, and Kelly, and
to my favorite readers, Cecilia, Madeleine, and Alex. —DJC

To my daughters Laura and Katherine, for whom reading
is as necessary as food and drink. —NDK

Acknowledgments

This book has been a collaborative effort by the three authors. Each author has actively contributed
to every chapter. We want to acknowledge the importance of each of us to the others. Working
collaboratively in separate parts of the country can be challenging, but we shared a vision and the
work went smoothly.

We are grateful to the students, classroom teachers, and colleagues with whom we have
worked during our careers—each of them has influenced what we have said here.

We extend special thanks to Lynne Greenwood, Language Arts and Literacy Specialist at the
Utah State Department of Education, and Jean Osborn, eminent reading expert from the Center
for the Study of Reading at the University of Illinois, for their comments and suggestions, which
guided our final revisions. We also thank Margery Rosnick, Acquisitions Editor, who brought us to
Scholastic and this series, and Ray Coutu, Development Editor at Scholastic, whose practical
support and constructive advice helped shape the final manuscript. We especially thank Margery
and Ray for their friendship.

We give our sincere appreciation to MaryEllen Vogt for her kind words regarding this book.
Finally, we thank friends and family members who allowed the writing of this book to take
precedence for a time. Such support is invaluable.

Cover and interior design by Maria Lilja
Cover photos: Tom Stewart/Corbis, Taxi/Getty Images, and Image 100/Getty Images
Interior photos by Maria Lilja unless otherwise noted
Interior Illustrations by Mike Reed

ISBN 0-439-61659-X

Contents

Foreword

Despite the best efforts of many teachers, reading specialists, and administrators, we still have many struggling readers in our classrooms. In the past, these students were consigned to special reading classes and low-track content classes in the hope that their literacy deficiencies could be remediated. However, this approach seldom had the desired effect, in part because few teachers had adequate training in how to provide appropriate reading instruction based upon students' diagnosed strengths and needs. Additionally, remedial reading programs were designed to treat students' literacy problems after the fact—by the time children were identified as needing help, they were often in deep academic trouble, demonstrating behaviors that often accompany reading failure, such as an intense dislike of school, low self-esteem, poor grades, limited participation in school activities, and inappropriate conduct. For these struggling readers, the die was cast and it was highly unlikely that they would ever exit their low-track groups and classes to join the mainstream. Not surprisingly, their drop-out rate was high.

Today, in an era of school reform as manifested in the No Child Left Behind and Reading First legislation, there is the expectation that *all* students will meet rigorous academic standards. Classroom teachers are expected to identify potential reading difficulties before they become damaging and lifelong. In a nutshell, this means that teachers must know how to diagnose their students' reading and writing strengths and weaknesses, and then use the assessment data to plan effective literacy instruction. While this may sound like a simple task, we all know, it is not. Standardized tests, though easy to administer, do not provide the information teachers need to make purposeful instructional decisions. Instead, what is needed in addition to a clear understanding of how children learn to read is a repertoire of proven diagnostic assessment tools, along with instructional approaches and methods that target specific areas of assessed need.

J. David Cooper, David Chard, and Nancy Kiger have filled this need by writing a unique book for teachers and administrators who share a hopeful vision for helping struggling readers overcome their difficulties. Rather than advocating "remediation," these knowledgeable and experienced educators suggest that prevention of reading problems and intervention are best accomplished when teachers use their systematic Prevention-Intervention Framework, which is made up of the following five components: assess and diagnose, teach/reteach, practice, apply, and reassess.

Each chapter opens with a comprehensive review of essential information about its focus, and a realistic classroom scenario that sets the stage for what follows. From there, the authors present a variety of proven assessments, instructional methods, and activities that are introduced through the steps of the Prevention-Intervention Framework. By following the steps, teachers will learn how to diagnose their students' reading development as it relates to oral language, phonemic awareness, phonics knowledge, word recognition, fluency, comprehension, and writing, and carry out effective instructional activities for each of these topics. They have selected some familiar approaches such as Reciprocal Teaching, as well as a number of new methods for preventing children's reading problems and intervening when they've occurred.

Looking back on my own teaching of remedial reading classes, I realize how much more effective my intervention would have been with a resource such as *The Struggling Reader*. Its conversational tone, applicability, and easy-to-use and varied assessments and activities set it apart from other books in the field. I encourage you to use it thoughtfully and purposefully. Follow the authors' Prevention-Intervention Framework for effective teaching. In so doing, you will scaffold your struggling readers and enable them to become independent and capable readers and writers.

—MARYELLEN VOGT, *California State University, Long Beach*
Past President, International Reading Association (2004-2005)

Introduction

Growing up as a struggling reader can have devastating consequences. That's why thinking about the needs of struggling readers keeps teachers awake at night. Despite our best efforts, some students continue to challenge us. When we look at research studies, periodicals, and professional books, we find no simple answer. If there were one, we'd all just apply it and move on.

Each of us has had struggling readers in our classrooms. Each of us has seen teachers work with struggling readers. Each of us has been asked, "What can we do?" by teachers, administrators, and families. This book is an attempt to answer that question by providing a simple, research-based framework that works.

Who We Are

Together, we three authors have more than 100 years of experience teaching struggling readers, using procedures that we, as researchers, have developed and tested.

Between us, we have taught preschool, elementary school, middle school, Title I, adult basic education, exceptional education, junior high school, high school, undergraduates, and graduate students in teacher training. We have been consultants, presenters, writers, researchers, and editors for reading programs and materials. We have worked in all 50 states and in more than eight countries.

We have taught in rural, suburban, and urban settings; in affluent communities and communities where most students were on free lunch programs; and in developing countries. We have worked with students whose first language is not English, whose lives are safest during the hours they are at school, whose families can't or don't read and write. So we are well qualified to address how to help struggling readers of all kinds.

Our book is not a collection of isolated activities. It is not a bag of tricks. It is not about gimmicks, or computer tracking, or packaged remedies. Rather, it is a framework for finding out what kids need to learn, planning instruction to meet those needs, and providing that instruction consistently, explicitly, and repeatedly until those needs are met. It will help you reach students who:

- struggle to read and write,

- do not thrive with the "regular" reading instruction that serves most students well,

- are in danger of falling farther and farther behind their peers,

- fall through the cracks daily,

- need to make more than adequate yearly progress in order to catch up, and/or

- may be discouraged and ready to give up.

Nothing motivates students to read like knowing how to read. Nothing helps students learn to read like good instruction. So use this framework. Ask questions. Look for additional ideas. And you will help your struggling readers make more than adequate yearly progress.

—JDC, DJC, NDK

CHAPTER 1

A Prevention-Intervention Framework

CASE STUDY

Today we are visiting two first-grade classrooms. As you watch what is happening, think about how these classrooms are alike and how they are different.

Rosa Vela's Classroom

Rosa Vela has 17 first graders—ten boys and seven girls. Four of her students speak Spanish fluently and understand a little English, three speak Haitian Creole and English, and the remaining ten speak English only. Ms. Vela has the children gathered around her on the carpet in the listening center and is showing them a photograph of a street in their neighborhood. She points to and names items in the photo such as apartment building, car, tree, trash can, and bus. The children repeat each word after her. She then asks individual children to point to items in the photo and name them. She goes on to describe activities that are taking place in the photo, such as a person getting on the bus. The children repeat after her and then take turns describing other things they see happening.

After the activity is finished, ten boys and girls move to centers around the room to listen to tapes and categorize pictures. The remaining seven children stay with Ms. Vela for reteaching of the sound for the letter *b*. She slowly pronounces words such as *bus* and *building*, emphasizing the sound of the first letter in both words. She gives the name of the letter and the sound it stands for: "*b*, /b/." After modeling this process several times, she says other words and has children give the beginning sounds. After about six minutes, she calls the entire class back to the rug.

Ms. Vela shows children the Big Book *Feathers for Lunch* (Ehlert, 1993), and they clap their hands and smile. She tells them they are going to reread the story and take turns putting events in order in the pocket chart. She reminds the children to use the sounds that they have been learning—/f/, /l/, /t/, and /b/—to help them read some of the words in the book. Ms. Vela models good reading by reading the text aloud. When she comes to words containing sounds that have been taught, she slows down and shows how she would use her knowledge to blend the sounds together and read the word. The entire group reads the book aloud, page by page. Then Ms. Vela calls on individual students to read a page and model reading the words with the sounds they have been learning.

When they're finished, seven children go across the hall to a reading specialist for 30 minutes of additional instruction. Ms. Vela tells us that the instruction children receive out of the room supports what

Focus of This Book

We have written this text for elementary or middle-school classroom teachers, reading specialists, and special-education teachers who have students who are struggling readers or who are at risk of becoming struggling readers. As we said in the introduction, it is not a collection of isolated activities, but rather a handbook that presents strategies and procedures that are based on reliable research and have been used successfully to prevent reading problems or to help students overcome them. We organize those strategies and procedures around a simple framework that will help you plan and carry out instruction.

NOTE: Definitions of boldfaced, italicized words appear in the glossary beginning on page 200.

she is doing in the room. While the group is gone, some children continue to practice sounds they have been learning, while others practice fluent reading by rereading little books with a partner.

Connie Barrera's Classroom

Across the hall we visit Connie Barrera's first grade. She has the same number of students as Ms. Vela and her class makeup and characteristics are similar. The children are completing a worksheet that requires them to circle pictures that begin with the same sound as the picture at the top of the page. They have several of these worksheets to complete.

As the children work, Ms. Barrera calls five or six of them at a time for group instruction. All groups use the same book. The children take turns reading sentences and/or pages aloud from the same book. We notice that some children in the group do not get a turn to read. After the reading, each group is given a worksheet that requires them to cut apart pictures of key events in the story and arrange them in the order in which they happened.

After all groups have met with Ms. Barrera and have completed the follow-up assignment, she collects the papers and explains to us that she will check them during her lunch break. We ask Ms. Barrera if any of her children work with the reading specialist. She says no, because they don't benefit from being away from her class.

These two brief classroom visits give us a snapshot of how varied first-grade instruction can be in the same school. How were these teachers' programs alike and how were they different? Take a moment to jot down your thoughts and then compare them to ours in Figure 1.1.

Though they have similar students and similar goals, Ms. Vela and Ms. Barrera are running two very different classrooms. Both have potential struggling readers but only Ms. Vela's children are receiving instruction designed to prevent them from becoming struggling readers—instruction that addresses each student's individual needs. All of her students are receiving the regular classroom instruction along with additional, individualized instruction

Rosa Vela's Class	Things in Common	Connie Barrera's Class
• Focus on language needs • Listening to sounds (phonemic awareness) • Systematic teaching of sounds • Additional help for students	• Class size • Class makeup • Potential struggling readers • Purpose: phonics and sequence	• No focus on language needs • No phonemic awareness • No direct teaching of sounds • No additional help for children

FIGURE 1.1 Comparison of Ms. Vela and Ms. Barrera's classes

to help them learn to read. Ms. Vela is using many of the strategies and techniques that are presented in this text.

Ms. Barrera, on the other hand, is basically providing all of her students with the same type of instruction with no attention to individual needs, which means, unfortunately, that some of her students are likely to become struggling readers.

Defining Struggling Readers

A *struggling reader* is a student who is experiencing significant difficulty learning to read. Most struggling readers are likely to exhibit difficulties in one or more of these areas (Chall & Curtis, 2003):

- Background experiences
- Oral language
- Decoding, including phonemic awareness and phonics knowledge
- Fluency
- Oral, reading, and writing vocabulary
- Comprehension
- Maintaining attention
- Motivation

Students Are Motivated to Read When They Are Taught How to Read

Motivation plagues most students who struggle to read—and their teachers. In fact, many students start out with high motivation but persistent failure causes them to lose it. Since individuals tend to be motivated when they are doing things they are good at doing, we believe that the best way to motivate struggling readers to read is to teach them how to read. In this sense, this entire book is about motivation. Teach struggling readers to read and they will read.

Gimmicks, contests, and rewards may temporarily motivate a struggling reader, but they don't work in the long run. No gimmick, contest, or reward can motivate students to do what they are unable to do. We have seen this nearly every day throughout our careers. As students learn how to read, they become motivated readers.

- Vision, hearing, or other physical ability necessary for processing text

No two struggling readers are exactly the same. Some may have difficulty decoding words. Others may have no problem decoding the words, but have difficulty understanding the author's message. Still others may struggle because they are unfamiliar with English language structures. Now for the good news: We can identify potential struggling readers before problems like these develop, and intervene if problems are already present (Snow, Burns, & Griffin, 1998). Therefore, to help a struggling reader or a potential struggling reader, programs should focus on prevention and intervention, as opposed to remediation.

Defining Remediation, Intervention, and Prevention

For many years, our approach to helping students with reading difficulties was to assign them to a remedial reading program. *Remediation* is the process of correcting a deficiency (*The American Heritage Dictionary*, 1992). Remedial reading programs usually identified skill weaknesses of students and then attempted to correct these problems. But these programs have not been successful (Allington & Walmsley, 1995). The students enrolled in them keep returning year after year, proving that once a student is labeled "remedial," he or she tends to remain remedial.

Think of your car. If you take a remedial approach to maintaining it, you wait until a problem occurs and then try to get it fixed. You don't take the car in for regularly scheduled maintenance. If your water pump fails while on a trip, you may bring the car in for repair only to discover a slew of other problems that led to the pump's malfunction—problems that could have been avoided if you had brought the car in for regularly scheduled maintenance. Of course, children's literacy development is much more complex and important than automobile maintenance. However, the fact is that remediation of reading problems has been no more successful than remediation of car problems. Therefore, researchers have come to focus on a different type of instruction known as intervention.

Intervention is the process of coming into or between so as to hinder or alter an action (*The American Heritage Dictionary*, 1992). A reading intervention program is one that prevents or stops failure by providing instruction beyond what is being provided in the core classroom program. Intervention may be provided on a day-to-day basis in the classroom or may be provided as a special program in the classroom or outside the classroom. This instruction should be provided by a certified teacher. Throughout this book we focus on some of the most effective reading interventions for preventing or stopping reading failure (Hiebert & Taylor, 1994; Pikulski, 1994).

Think about your car again. If you take an intervention approach to maintaining it, you pay attention to all warning lights and gauges. If the temperature gauge shows the engine is hot, you immediately have it checked. On the other hand, in order to prevent car problems, you take it in for regular, thorough maintenance. Likewise, to prevent reading problems, you must take a prevention perspective when it comes to instruction.

Prevention is the process of keeping something from happening (*The American Heritage Dictionary*, 1992). Prevention in reading instruction means setting up conditions that stop potential struggling readers from becoming struggling readers. We do this to some degree by providing sound core classroom instruction and intervention as needed—instruction that builds a solid foundation that helps struggling readers and potential struggling readers learn to read, plus many opportunities to read and to use what they have learned (Allington, 2001; Cunningham & Allington, 2003). Think back to your car. If you take a prevention approach, you provide all of the regularly scheduled service. Everything is checked, with the hope that problems will never occur.

There is a greater likelihood that potential struggling readers will not develop into struggling readers if they are given quality core instruction, and prevention and intervention when the signs indicate the need. Throughout this book we focus on strategies for noticing these signs and providing prevention and intervention based on what you see.

A Framework for Core Instruction—Prevention and Intervention

Students who are or show signs of becoming struggling readers cannot make adequate progress with regular instruction alone. We cannot simply wait and hope for the best; instead, we need to take steps to support the struggling readers through systematic teaching. Figure 1.2 presents a framework for planning and providing core instruction and intervention. We use this framework throughout the book to organize each chapter's content, incorporating all the assessment tools and teaching strategies you need in order to work with students on decoding, comprehension, fluency, and other important areas of literacy.

1. Assess and Diagnose

During this step, you find out how well the student is performing in the area of concern. This assessment may involve the use of standardized tests, informal measures, teacher observations, or a combination of the three. If your assessment and diagnosis reveal a problem that is beyond the scope of your skills, confer with specialists in your district. Throughout the handbook, we give suggestions for assessment and diagnosis.

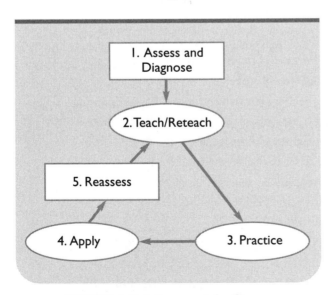

FIGURE 1.2 A Framework for Core Instruction—Prevention and Intervention

2. Teach/Reteach

In this step, you usually provide explicit, direct instruction in the strategy, skill, or process that the student needs, based on your assessment and diagnosis. We encourage you to model the strategy, skill, or process for the student, providing multiple examples as needed. Sometimes the instruction you provide will be more student-centered and less teacher-directed. For example, post-reading discussion groups is a student-centered way to help a student who is struggling with comprehension.

3. Practice

This phase is when you provide students with multiple opportunities to use what has been taught under teacher direction. Practice will vary according to the type of strategy, skill, or process that has been taught. Practice should be both teacher-guided and independent.

4. Apply

In this phase, students read and use a strategy, skill, or process independently. This may involve reading of words, sentences, or longer text, depending on what has been taught. Keep in mind that the goal is to get struggling readers to use the skills, strategies, and processes on their own as they read.

5. Reassess

At this point, you reassess to make certain that the student has learned what you taught. Most of the assessment should take place after the student has applied the skill, strategy, or process, but some of it may also occur during the Apply step through observation of how the student uses the strategy or skill in question. What you learn from the assessment will help you determine whether to move on to a new area or to continue working on the current one.

In the chapters that follow, we provide you with many examples of how to use this framework, focusing on areas in which struggling readers are likely to require instruction. (See Figure 1.3.) Do not feel that you must read the chapters in order. If you like, read only those that address the specific needs of your students. The last chapter offers many suggestions for keeping yourself current with the professional literature and research on helping struggling readers.

Chapter Focus

2	Oral Language
3	Phonemic Awareness
4	Word Recognition
5	Meaning Vocabulary
6	Reading Fluency
7	Comprehension
8	Writing for Struggling Readers
9	Keeping Yourself Current

FIGURE 1.3
Overview of chapters

CHAPTER 2

Oral Language

Today we are observing a conversation between two teachers about Justin, a first-grade student who is experiencing language difficulties. Joellen Carter is Justin's teacher. Rich Olson is a speech-language pathologist with whom Ms. Carter is consulting because of her concern about Justin.

Ms. Carter tells Mr. Olson that Justin has just entered her first-grade classroom, two months after school has begun. She has talked with Justin's foster mother, who does not know much about his early childhood life except that he did not attend preschool.

Mr. Olson asks Ms. Carter to describe what led her to ask for help from him. Here is an excerpt of their conversation.

MS. CARTER: From the first day Justin was in the classroom, I noticed that he didn't talk as much as the other children and when he did talk, it sounded like baby-talk.

MR. OLSON: Can you give me an example?

MS. CARTER: When Justin wants something, he says, "Me want it." And he refers to himself by his name—"Justin wants lunch." He doesn't use the pronoun "I."

CASE STUDY

MR. OLSON:	Tell me about his behavior and speech when you are reading or talking about a story you have read to the class.
MS. CARTER:	He hasn't begun reading at all—he recognizes only his own name in print. Also, when I asked him what his favorite stories are, he couldn't name even one. When the class recites nursery rhymes together, Justin doesn't participate—he doesn't seem to know the words.
MR. OLSON:	Tell me something about how he interacts with the other children.
MS. CARTER:	He doesn't interact very much. When he's in a group of children in a center or at recess, he never says anything unless another child asks him a direct question. Then he usually answers with just a single word. In fact, the only time he voluntarily says something is when he needs to use the bathroom. It's almost like he can only use words to take care of his basic needs. He doesn't seem to know how to have a conversation.
MR. OLSON:	Well, from what you tell me, it seems that Justin's language development is delayed. He may need further help from me, but let's talk about what you can do to help his oral language development. As his language improves, I think you'll see him begin to make sense of print.

When we speak of oral language development, we are referring to children's emerging ability to speak and listen. By the time most children arrive at elementary school, their oral language is strong—they are able to understand and communicate basic ideas and feelings clearly. However, some students, like Justin, come to school with delays—delays that could lead to problems in reading and writing later (Snow et al., 1998; Hart & Risley, 1995). In this chapter we focus on how oral language develops, how it relates to learning to read and write, and how you can help students who are experiencing difficulties.

First, we discuss three major components of language, *form*, *content*, and *function*, and how they contribute to a child's ability to learn to read and write.

Form This includes the sounds in words (*phonology*), the meaningful parts of words such as base words or prefixes (*morphology*), and the order in which we use words (*syntax*). Can the child hear and produce the sounds of our language, add endings to create word forms such as plurals, use tone and pitch to add meaning, and use words in the correct order to produce a sentence?

Content This includes vocabulary, or the words we use, and semantics, or the knowledge of what the words mean. Does the child have in his oral language many of the words he is likely to meet when he begins to read? Does he know the words he needs in order to express his feelings and his needs and to have conversations with others? Does he understand what he hears?

Function This refers to how and why we use language—for what purpose. Does the child use language to make himself understood? Does he use language to request, explain, direct, persuade, and so forth?

Next, we show how to weave instruction in oral language into your systematic plan of prevention and intervention. We present a sample oral language lesson designed to help struggling speakers—students who are likely to become struggling readers.

Finally, we suggest several activities that can be carried out in your classroom routinely and frequently to stimulate oral language growth.

The Components of Oral Language

Language is a system of codes developed as a conventional way to communicate ideas and feelings. Let's look at each of the three primary components of oral language in more detail and at how they relate to learning to read and write.

Form

This component relates to the physical aspects of language and is made up of three major parts: phonology, morphology, and syntax.

Phonology refers to the sound system of language. This includes the *phonemes*, or sounds that make up words, as well as *prosody*, the ability to use language features such as tone, stress, and pitch to convey meaning.

Being able to make use of the individual sounds in words (and eventually the letters that stand for these sounds) is clearly tied to learning to read, which involves recognizing letters and combinations of letters in print and saying the sounds. Students who struggle with the sounds in words usually struggle with reading and writing later. Chapter 3 deals in detail with phonological and phonemic awareness, identifying and producing individual word sounds. Chapter 4 deals with *phonics*—connecting sounds to symbols—or phonology and *orthography*. Chapter 8 deals with writing.

When we speak, we convey meaning using more than just the words. We use prosody. We stress some words more than others; our voice may rise to a shout or drop to a whisper. We may pause between two words, changing the meaning slightly. A simple question such as "What are you doing?" can have different meanings depending on the tone in which it is asked. Students who have not acquired the use of prosody may fail to recognize that they are meant to "hear" the stress, tone, and pitch of written words when reading or being read to. Without this ability, their comprehension may break down (Beck, McKeown, & Kucan, 2002).

Morphology has to do with the meaningful parts of words. A *morpheme* is the smallest meaningful part of a word. There are two kinds of morphemes: free (or unbound) and bound. A *free morpheme* can stand alone. The words *trap*, *sun*, *light*, and *drink* are examples of free morphemes. A *bound morpheme* cannot stand alone; it must be attached to a free morpheme to have meaning. The suffixes *er*, *y*, and *ing* are examples of bound morphemes because they do not have meaning unless they are attached to a free morpheme. Often a spelling change occurs in the free morpheme when a bound morpheme is attached to it, as in *trapper* and *sunny*.

As oral language develops, children acquire skill in using the morphology of their language. Young children often overgeneralize. For example, as they begin to learn how to pluralize words, you'll hear delightful "mistakes" such as *sockes* and *mans*. As they grow, children acquire conventional morphology and begin to say *socks* and *men* and use language correctly.

Syntax refers to the rules that govern how we organize words into sentences. Little children may use two-word phrases such as "Justin drink." By age two, most children can put together a complete sentence: "I want a drink, please." As children mature, they begin to use even more complex sentences: "I'd prefer a glass of milk if you have it, but water would be fine." As students listen, read, and write, their awareness and use of increasingly complex syntax grows.

Syntax may be a stumbling block for students whose first language is not English. Other languages may use words in a different order. For example, in Spanish an adjective follows a noun rather than preceding it.

Our knowledge of syntax helps us to comprehend what we read and to read fluently. Chapter 6 deals with fluency and Chapter 7 deals with comprehension. Here we give only an example of how a reader's knowledge of syntax affects reading. As we read a sentence, we automatically know what kind of word needs to go in which slot in the sentence. For example, let's say you come across this sentence: "There must have been a hundred _____ in the sky last night." You know what kind of word belongs in the blank (i.e., a thing), even if you don't know what part of speech it is. If you had to guess, you'd probably say a noun and choose one that makes sense in the context of the sentence: it has to be something that is seen at night, is in the sky, and is present in large quantities.

As a proficient reader, you know the missing word is most likely *stars*. But even if we told you it was a made-up word, say "vobaltics," you would infer its meaning because of your knowledge of syntax and context.

We need to help struggling readers use their knowledge of syntax to supply the right kind of word in a particular place in a sentence, even if they don't know what the word means if they do decode it. As they use more complex sentences orally, they will be able to read more complex sentences without getting lost.

Content

Content is related to the **vocabulary** and semantics that make up language. We consider the rate at which students learn new words, their ability to understand multiple meanings of words, and their ability to understand the relationships among words. We know that students learn approximately 3,000 new words per year (White, Graves, & Slater, 1990). We also know that students extend and learn variations on single words—or, as Stahl (2004) calls it, the nature of individual word knowledge. For example, when a learner is first exposed to the word *cow*, she may understand it as a kind of animal. Later, that learner may come to know more specifically what makes a cow a cow (gives milk, eats grass, says "moo") and be able to name characteristics that distinguish it from other four-legged animals. Still later, that learner may discover that the word *cow* is also a verb that has nothing at all to do with animals.

When we read, we use our speaking and listening vocabularies to comprehend the text. So, naturally, if those vocabularies do not contain words we encounter in the text, we're going to have problems understanding the author's message. For example, a young reader may meet the word *basement* and be able to decode it and pronounce it. But if the child has no experience with basements and doesn't know what one is—in other words, if the word isn't in that child's oral language—he has no way to confirm that he has said the correct word.

For older readers, decoding is more apt to be a problem than lack of vocabulary. That is, if they could just learn to decode the symbols, the word they say will trigger a word that is already in their oral language. In fact, for competent readers beyond third grade, reading is the greatest source of new vocabulary. Clearly, the more we can help students develop oral language, the more words they will understand when they meet them in print. Meaning vocabulary—understanding what words mean when heard or read—is the topic of Chapter 5.

Children use language
to share ideas.

Function

Function refers to *pragmatics*, or the way a speaker communicates. Before entering school, children use oral language mostly for functional purposes, such as to get food or attention. They go from gestures and one-word grunts to complex sentences such as "I want to get up now, please." By school age, most children's oral language has moved beyond function into telling stories, responding to questions, exchanging ideas, or expressing feelings.

A child's ability to understand and use oral language will affect his or her ability to understand written text. As students read, they need to interpret the author's words. They need to go beyond saying and understanding the meaning of each word. They need to be able to put the words together in their minds and "get it." The student who just isn't interested in reading or doesn't want to try would be helped by further development in oral language. Over time, students will be able to comprehend written text that is more complex than their oral language. As students learn to read and write, oral language development plays a critical part.

Applying the Intervention Framework to Oral Language

As we have discussed in the first half of this chapter, the relationship between oral language and literacy is complex but clear. So it's critical to implement a well-designed oral language program that includes:

- explicit instruction in important language concepts and skills such as syntax, oral vocabulary, and prosody;
- carefully sequenced opportunities for learning;
- application of newly learned language concepts;
- integrated review of concepts and skills as new ones are learned;
- language activities; and
- continual and systematic assessment.

To help you do this, we will use the framework introduced in Chapter 1 to show how to identify problems in your struggling readers that may be related to oral language and then take steps to overcome them. We start by discussing each of the steps in the framework as it relates to oral language development and struggling readers. Next, we present a sample lesson, and finally, we include several activities that support and stimulate oral language development.

Assess and Diagnose

Early in the school year, you can assess your students' oral language informally, using anecdotal records, individual conferences, or whole-class or small-group discussions. If, by carrying out assessments like those, you suspect a child may have difficulties, as Ms. Carter did with Justin, use a checklist like the one in Figure 2.1, which is organized around the three language components described earlier in this chapter—form, content, and function. If Ms. Carter had used this checklist, she would be able to report specific areas of difficulty to the specialist and plan more focused instruction for Justin. The checklist would probably have revealed that Justin had difficulty in language use and vocabulary.

Notice that there are places to make several observations, enabling Ms. Carter to tell whether a behavior previously absent is now present, such as syntax or prosody. She might make up her own checklist to target just the areas she wants to observe closely in Justin's oral language. Those observations will help her plan specific teaching strategies to enhance his oral language growth.

If your assessment indicates problems, you may want to confer with a language development specialist. Your observations will help him or her determine whether the child is, in fact, experiencing a problem with oral language and, if so, whether that problem can be resolved in the classroom, outside the classroom, or in both places.

Teach/Reteach

While much of oral language develops naturally, for children with language difficulties, specific instruction is needed. As examples, we'll discuss two common problems associated with struggling readers.

A common barrier to comprehension for struggling readers is lack of background experiences or prior knowledge. This doesn't mean that these children haven't had enough experiences; more likely, their background experiences don't match school expectations. They may not be familiar with the stories most children know. They may have trouble relating to a story about a traditional family because they have never been part of one. They may not know enough about living in a city, working on a farm, riding in an airplane, or hearing a live concert to understand when listening to or reading stories about those activities. Part of our job is to determine what students already know about a topic and whether they have the necessary vocabulary to understand it and discuss it.

OBSERVATION CHECKLIST
Oral Language

+ BEHAVIOR PRESENT
- BEHAVIOR ABSENT
/ BEHAVIOR SOMEWHAT PRESENT

Name_____ Grade _____ Age _____

Specific Language Behaviors	Dates Observed						Comments
Language Form							
Speaks with appropriate pace							
Uses appropriate syntax							
Self-corrects when nonstandard forms are used							
Language Content							
Uses new vocabulary introduced through instruction in appropriate contexts							
Recognizes pronoun referents							
Shows increased vocabulary							
Asks for meanings of unknown words							
Language Function/Use							
Responds to questions about previously taught concepts or previously read stories							
Uses language appropriately to communicate a purpose (e.g., wants, information, story retell)							
Listens and paraphrases							
Participates in discussion							
Asks questions							

Additional Comments:

FIGURE 2.1 An observation checklist to assess oral language

The Struggling Reader: Interventions That Work

How to teach meaning vocabulary and link it to background is addressed in detail in Chapter 5 and Chapter 7.

Another problem that we commonly see among struggling readers, which has implications for teaching, is their ability to deal with pronoun referents. For example, if while speaking or listening, a student has trouble understanding who is referred to by "she" or what is meant by "it," then that student is apt to have the same trouble while reading. Oral language lessons that focus on identifying pronoun referents, like the one we present later in this chapter, will help a struggling reader deal with them in print.

Practice

Whether we're teaching reading, writing, math, science, or social studies, students need time to practice the skills we expect them to master. The same is true for oral language. The more students practice new uses of oral language, such as paraphrasing a part of a story or demonstrating appropriate intonation, the more likely they will be able to apply those uses later to their reading and writing. Later in this chapter, we suggest activities that can be used to provide practice.

Apply

While practice is focused on a particular skill, applying that skill means using it while in the process of carrying out a broader task. Sometimes educators use the term *authentic* to describe such a task. So, if you have taught your students an aspect of oral language such as how to express past tense, and have provided specific practice on the skill, be sure to also engage students in oral language experiences, such as a discussion of a trip they have made or a film they have watched, in which they will need to use past-tense verbs.

Reassess

The final step of the intervention framework helps you decide whether a student needs further teaching in the area that you identified in the first assessment. You may assess during the Apply step in many cases. In other words, once you've taught a student how to change a verb to its past tense, you can begin to assess whether he has learned to do this when he tries to apply it to subsequent examples you provide. With oral language, you may need to assess both oral language during class discussion and the transfer of a newfound oral language ability to reading.

Sample Lessons Using the Intervention Framework With Struggling Primary and Intermediate Students: Identifying Pronoun Referents

This lesson focuses on identifying pronoun referents. For each step you'll see how the lesson might be carried out for primary and intermediate students.

Assess and Diagnose

Prepare two-part statements and questions that include the pronoun in the first part and the pronoun referent in the second part. Read both sentences and the question aloud and ask students to answer the question. Here are some samples.

Primary Assessment

1. Jim threw the ball. Sally caught it. What does the word *it* refer to? (the ball)

2. Maria crawled under the covers. She was very sleepy. What does *she* refer to? (Maria)

3. The children went to the park. They had a good time. What does *they* refer to? (the children)

4. The monkeys were making faces. All the children laughed at them. What does *them* refer to? (the monkeys)

Intermediate Assessment

1. A photographer took a picture of my whole family. We thought it was a terrible picture. What does *we* refer to? (you and your family)

2. Wind and rain had carved the rocks into beautiful works of art. I guess they aren't always destructive, are they? What does *they* refer to? (wind and rain)

3. Jillian and Dad spent two days in Florida. Jillian especially loved its beaches. What does *its* refer to? (Florida's)

4. Jeremy went online to research information about the election. There was way too much to look at. Nevertheless, he chose the most likely listing and clicked on it. What does *he* refer to? (Jeremy) What does *it* refer to? (the most likely listing)

Uncertainty about any of the pronoun referents indicates that students need instruction in that area.

If you want to further assess whether students are using and understanding pronoun referents in their oral language, listen to them carefully during group and one-on-one conversations. With first graders, you may notice the immature use of pronouns, as when Justin said, "Me want it."

Teach/Reteach

Model pronoun referents by reading aloud sentences that you construct or take from a book. First read the text aloud for fun; then read it again, stopping at pronouns to help students think about to what or whom they refer. Once students are able to pinpoint the referents to pronouns that you identify, have them identify pronouns on their own and continue to pinpoint referents. In other words, gradually release to students responsibility for the task. Here's an example of what that might look like in an intermediate classroom, using a short paragraph that you might have created.

> Taking Spike to the vet was always tough for Joe, but he needed his flea shot and he needed his toenails clipped. Joe snapped the leash onto Spike's collar and gave a little jerk. He felt him resist, digging his claws into the floor. "I know, I know. You hate it! Don't worry—we'll be home soon and I'll give you a treat."

TEACHER: It says "he needed his flea shot. . . ." Who is "he"?

STUDENT: Joe.

TEACHER: Why do you think that?

STUDENT: That's the last person named right before the pronoun "he."

TEACHER: That's logical thinking, but go a little further—listen to the whole passage again. [*Reread passage.*]

STUDENT: Oh, I see—"he" is Spike.

TEACHER: And how do you know that?

STUDENT: The sentence goes on to talk about things that a vet does for a pet.

With primary students, choose or create a story appropriate for their age and follow the same process.

Practice

Because this is an oral language lesson, you cannot rely on tasks students do at their desks independently. They need to be speaking. However, opportunities for identifying pronoun referents will arise during any school day. To pave the way, you may write on a chart or the chalkboard a morning message each morning that contains pronoun referents, such as:

> Today is Marvin's birthday.
> Marvin is the class hamster.
> He was a gift from Scott Lee.
> We will celebrate his birthday all day.

First read the sentences aloud to or with your students. Then ask them to identify who "he" is in the third sentence. Continue talking about the pronouns in the last sentence and why it's important to be able to identify pronouns and pronoun referents while speaking, listening, reading, and writing.

Throughout the day, look for opportunities to call attention to pronouns in oral language, during conversations, oral-report readings, or Read Aloud time. This will reinforce students' understanding of pronoun referents.

Apply

The application of student understanding of pronoun referents as a part of oral language is in their response to what they hear. Therefore, you can infer application of the skill when children understand to what or to whom a pronoun refers without your having to guide them.

As struggling readers deal with pronouns in written text, help them make the connection to the oral language lessons they have been taught. Call attention to pronouns in written text; remind students that knowing what the pronoun stands for improves their understanding when they listen; ask them to apply that same kind of logical thinking in order to understand the pronoun referents they encounter as they read.

Reassess

Construct more two-part statements and questions like those used for your initial assessment. If students continue to have problems identifying pronoun referents, reteach. If they don't, move to the next lesson on referents, perhaps using appropriate pronouns in speech and then using them in writing.

Activities to Support Oral Language Development in Struggling Readers

Oral language cannot develop in a silent classroom. Children need to be surrounded by spoken language in order to develop their own language. The activities we suggest below are a few ways to support and encourage oral language development.

Talk

Students need time to talk to themselves, to each other, to you, and to other adults. When you talk with children, model what a real-life conversation is. Don't turn your conversation into a question-and-answer session, with you always asking the questions and the children expected to give a correct answer. The vocabulary you use should be familiar to the children, but stretch their minds a bit too. Use "big" words. Tell them interesting things you have heard or read about. Make conversation a real part of the day.

Older struggling readers need opportunities to engage in conversation too. During conversations with them, focus on their ideas, not on the language. Correcting grammar or pronunciation during natural conversation almost guarantees that a student will stop speaking.

Talk is critical for students who are learning English as a second language. By being immersed in language with you and with their classmates, those students begin to acquire the structures and vocabulary of English. Acquisition of oral language almost always precedes the ability to read and write in a second language (Snow et al., 1998; Hurley & Tinajero, 2001).

Talk in the classroom also gives you a chance to model standard usage for students. As mentioned earlier, interrupting and correcting nonstandard usage seldom has the desired effect. It is far better to listen to the student and rephrase his or her idea using correct form. Over time, you'll most likely begin to see students apply standard usage on their own, while speaking, reading, and writing.

Read Aloud

The benefits of reading aloud to students of all ages cannot be overstated. Through listening, students increase their understanding of how language works, add words to their vocabularies, and have models of accepted language use. When you read to students on a regular basis, you will hear the language of books in students' oral language and see it in their written language.

Your good oral reading will model prosody—or the effective use of stress, pitch, and tone. When you read with expression, students will too. Best of all, they will begin to use prosody naturally to convey meaning when they read aloud and speak.

Reading aloud also gives you a chance to talk about language with children. You can talk with them about words they hear and find interesting. You can talk about how to figure out what words mean while listening. You can talk about how an author uses words to provide information, give directions, tell a story, make you laugh or cry, or pique your curiosity. In fact, you can have exactly the same kinds of discussions about books students listen to as about those they read. The more comfortable they are talking about something they have heard, the more comfortable they'll be discussing something they have read.

Finally, reading aloud introduces students to written material they may not yet be able to read on their own and whets their appetite for the day they will be able to read it.

Dramatic Play

Students of all ages, even older students, enjoy turning favorite stories into plays. As students act out the story, they not only use the vocabulary and language forms of the story, but also practice prosody as they take on the role of a troll or a fairy godmother or a big, bad wolf.

Puppet Play

A student who never volunteers to speak in class might come to life when speaking through a puppet to tell about a family trip or a party, or while taking on a role in retelling a story. Puppets can be made from easy-to-find materials such as socks, construction paper, tongue depressors, or Styrofoam boxes.

Reciting Poems and Singing Songs

By teaching students to recite familiar poems and sing songs, you can help them gain pleasure in language. The rhythm and rhyme will aid in memory, and you can discuss how the words combine with the music to convey meaning. Make up motions to fit poems or songs. For example, if you're singing "The Wheels on the Bus," have students pretend to open the door, activate the wipers, and honk the horn at appropriate points.

Word Play

Play word games with children such as "I'm going to Grandma's house and I'm taking a _____ ." Use a spare minute or two during the day to play with words. You could have students stand in a circle, say a word such as *bat*, toss a beanbag to a child, and ask that child to give a word that rhymes with *bat*. That child then tosses the beanbag to a classmate for another word that rhymes with *bat*— or for an entirely new word to be rhymed.

Elaborate Sentences

When you respond to students, elaborate on the content of their sentences. By doing this, you introduce more complex sentence structures and new vocabulary. For example, if Tim says, "Look at my shirt," you may say, "Your shirt is gorgeous! Look at the plaid stripes making an intricate pattern. I think I see some burnt orange and a little forest green along with the white. Splendid!"

The activities suggested here will help students make the leap from oral language to print.

Conclusion

Whether a student learns to read and write with ease and confidence may depend on his or her oral language development. You must assess the oral language of each of your students in terms of form, content, and function. If you identify a problem, you must take steps to teach the oral language skills they need. With young children, such teaching may prevent reading problems from arising. With older students who are already struggling with reading, intervention to strengthen oral language will go a long way toward strengthening reading.

Phonemic Awareness

CASE STUDY

Gary Bensen is a kindergarten teacher who knows that observing children closely can make all the difference in preventing future problems. One of his students, 6-year-old Thomas, is unusually quiet. In fact, his voice is almost inaudible. Mr. Bensen knows that being able to hear sounds in words is a critical part of learning to read, but he has no idea whether Thomas is able to do this because he seldom speaks. Today, Mr. Bensen is doing his best to find out by informally assessing Thomas's ability to identify the sounds at the beginnings of words. He says one-syllable words such as *ball* and asks Thomas to isolate and then pronounce their beginning sounds. Thomas is successful with about half the words.

Next, Mr. Bensen asks Thomas to segment, or break apart, words into separate sounds. Thomas is able to do so for two words: *mat* and *can*. We can see Thomas getting frustrated trying to do what Mr. Bensen wants him to do. In time, he begins to just echo the words Mr. Bensen says without making any attempt to segment them. He seems close to tears.

We are pleased to see Mr. Bensen put down his list of words, give Thomas a big smile, and say, "We've done enough for now, don't you think? Let's take a break." Thomas wipes his eyes and smiles in relief.

Thomas has not yet acquired *phonemic awareness*, a common difficulty for struggling beginning readers. In this chapter we explain the concept of phonemic awareness, why it is important, how most children acquire it, and how to help struggling readers of any age who have not acquired it. We show you how to apply the intervention framework to phonemic awareness and develop lessons that will help struggling readers.

What Is Phonemic Awareness and Why Is It Important?

As very young children begin to use language, most show a growing awareness of the sounds of our language. They enjoy songs, nursery rhymes, and stories with lots of rhyming words, such as *The Cat in the Hat*. Soon, they begin playing with language, making up their own rhymes with real words, such as *cat* and *bat*, and nonsense words, such as *lat* and *zat*. They giggle as they change the sound at the beginning of words or at the end: *kitty, mitty, fitty,* and *bat, bam, bad*. This growing understanding that language is made up of discrete sounds is *phonological awareness* (Liberman, Shankweiler, & Liberman, 1989).

What Is Phonemic Awareness?

The ability to hear and isolate individual sounds in words is phonemic awareness. This happens before children associate letters with sounds. Without being taught, most young children grasp that language is used to express thoughts. Eventually they learn to identify individual words and then the syllables that make up those words. They can drag out the pronunciation of a word, clapping on each syllable. Then they learn to hear *onsets*—the initial consonant sound of a word—and *rimes*—the vowel and ending sound. For example, in the word *pack*, the /p/ is the onset and /ack/ is the rime. But hearing onsets and rimes isn't enough for children to become readers. They must be able to hear the individual sounds in words—the phonemes. The word *pack* is one syllable with three phonemes: the initial /p/, the vowel /a/, and the ending sound /k/ represented by two letters *ck* (Adams, 1990; Liberman, Shankweiler, Fischer, & Carter, 1974).

Frequently, phonemic awareness is confused with phonics. They are not the same, though phonemic awareness is a precursor to using phonics. Phonics involves more than being able to hear and produce phonemes in words. It involves knowing the letter or letters that stand for the phonemes, recognizing letters in print, and being able to associate the sound that those letters usually stand for. In other words, phonemic awareness is speech-based, whereas phonics is print-based. In this chapter we are concerned only with phonemic awareness. Phonics is discussed thoroughly in Chapter 4.

Why Is Phonemic Awareness Important?

To become literate, the child must grasp the **alphabetic principle**—which means that the sounds we hear in words in English can be represented by written symbols. Decoding, which is required for reading, involves looking at a print symbol and associating it with a sound. Encoding, which is required for writing, involves hearing a sound and knowing what symbol, or letter(s), to write to represent that sound.

Phonemic awareness is critical to both decoding and encoding. Here's why: Let's say a child who has acquired the alphabetic principle and phonemic awareness is reading and comes to the sentence, "The frog nabbed the fly with its long tongue." He can read almost every word in the sentence correctly, because he either recognizes it instantly or figures it out by associating sounds with the letters he sees. But the last word, *tongue*, stumps him. Sounding out each letter doesn't lead to a word that makes sense—or any word at all, for that matter. But, if the child can associate a couple of the letters with sounds (phonics), use information from the rest of the sentence to help him (context), and apply what he knows about frogs and flies (background knowledge), then he can probably figure out the last word. As he reads on, he will know whether he was correct.

When it comes to encoding or writing, children use phonemic awareness and their understanding of the alphabetic principle as they attempt to spell words. In the piece of student writing shown in Figure 3.1, many words are not spelled correctly. However, the writer is aware of the individual sounds in those words because he has used a symbol for each of those sounds; spelling attempts that are close to correct are called approximations.

Some students come to kindergarten without phonemic awareness—perhaps due to a lack of exposure to English or to standard English pronunciation, or perhaps as a result of ear infections, hearing difficulties, learning disabilities, or other factors (Shaywitz, 2003). So, when formal reading instruction begins, it may be hard for these children to associate sounds with symbols and blend sounds into words. These children need to be identified early so that steps can be taken to teach them what they have not yet learned.

When we do not identify early the children who need help, we risk delaying their learning for years. It may very well be that some children who are put into special classes might have caught on and caught up had their problems been identified early. In fact, some estimates suggest that approximately 90 percent of students identified as having learning disabilities lack phonemic awareness (Stanovich, 1986).

FIGURE 3.1 Children's early writing can help you assess their ability to hear sounds in their own vocabulary accurately.

"This is a story about an alligator. It got caught in a cage and struggled to get out. But he couldn't get out of the cage and finally he got out and he swam in the lake."

—Alex, age 6

How Do Learners Develop Phonemic Awareness?

Phonemic awareness begins from the moment a child begins his or her life. An infant hears the sounds of language. At first these sounds do not represent anything meaningful. Gradually, however, the infant associates meaning with the sounds and begins recognizing words such as *up*, *bottle*, *Daddy*, *Mommy*, *bedtime*, and *doggy*. In time, the child repeats these meaningful sounds, which prompts positive responses from the adults or other children around him. Those responses encourage him to experiment further with sounds.

At first, children don't isolate individual words, largely because of the way we use language. When we speak to young children we don't pause between each word. It isn't surprising, then, that children combine common phrases into single-word utterances, such as "Onceuponatime." Children who memorize songs or the Pledge of Allegiance sing or say the sounds without realizing that they are singing or saying individual, meaningful words. Gradually, that gets sorted out. Eventually, children can tell you the individual words in the piece.

Similarly, as children are learning the alphabet, they may run the names of the letters together so they sound like one continuous stream of sound. Eventually children learn that each letter has a name and begin separating the stream of sound into those names, though they may not yet know the role that knowledge will soon play in their lives as they learn to read and write.

Sharing books such as the one shown here can help children develop phonemic awareness.

The Struggling Reader: Interventions That Work

As children begin acquiring language, the adults in their lives usually pay more attention to whether a child uses the correct word than to the correct pronunciation of the word. For example, if a child sees a horse in a field and says "See cow!" a parent will undoubtedly correct him by saying something like, "No, that's not a cow. It's a horse." If the child is lucky, the parent will explain details to help the child remember how the two animals are different. If the child is very young and mispronounces the word, research shows that the parent will probably not correct him.

Later, we see phonological awareness developing as the child begins playing with the sounds of words. For example, he may say, "See cow!" The parent may say, "That's not a cow. It's a horsey." And the child may say: "horsey, morsey, dorsey, torsey!" Or "cow, now, vow, wow!" As that parent reads to the child from a rhyming book such as Dr. Seuss's *Green Eggs and Ham*, he or she can support this development by hesitating before saying the last word in a rhyme and giving the child time child to supply it. Moments like this are exciting because they show children are developing phonemic awareness. But not all children reach this stage before beginning school, so they need instruction.

How Do We Teach Phonemic Awareness to Struggling Readers?

Even though many children come to school with well-developed phonological and phonemic awareness, all kindergartners should receive formal instruction to ensure that they gain these essential understandings. Once your assessment reveals that students have these skills, this instruction should be discontinued. This instruction consists of a series of lessons, which should be conducted orally. Later in the chapter, we present a sample of how to teach one such lesson. Here is a possible sequence of activities, which should be incorporated into your lessons.

Activity #1:
- Segment sentences into words: *The cat has a hat. = The - cat - has - a - hat.*
- Blend words into a sentence: *The - cat - has - a - hat. = The cat has a hat.*

Activity #2:
- Segment compound words into separate words: *sidewalk = side + walk.*
- Blend words into a compound word: *side + walk = sidewalk.*

Activity #3:
- Segment two-syllable words that are not compounds: *sister = sis + ter*.
- Blend syllables into word: *sis + ter = sister*.

Activity #4:
- Segment words with more syllables: *neighborhood = neigh + bor + hood*.
- Blend syllables into word: *neigh + bor + hood = neighborhood*.

Activity #5:
- Segment words (and/or syllables) into onsets and rimes: *cat = /k/ /at/*.
- Blend segmented onsets and rimes into words: */k/ /at/ = cat*.

Activity #6:
- Segment words into individual phonemes: *cat = /k/ /a/ /t/*.
- Blend individual phonemes into words: */k/ /a/ /t/ = cat*.

Each of these activities must include your explicit modeling of the skill, followed by ample opportunities for your students to practice the skill with new words. Be sure to assess as you teach, so that you will know how quickly to introduce each new segmenting and blending skill. You probably notice that the activities ask for segmenting—taking a word apart—and then blending—putting it back together. This is intentional; research suggests that blending and segmenting are critical aspects of phonemic awareness that must be developed (Chard & Dickson, 1999). Depending on where your students are, you may decide to teach segmenting and blending in separate sessions or in single sessions. What's most important to remember is that lessons like these may have already been taught to your students without success. If this is the case, it's wiser to teach skills in smaller, more discrete steps in order to give students a chance to catch up.

Phonemic awareness lessons like these will help prevent later trouble in reading for some students. If the children do not respond to the lessons or seem frustrated by them, slow down or repeat. Most children have acquired phonemic awareness by the middle of first grade. With older struggling readers, you will teach such lessons only to those who are still struggling with it. However, do continue them with children who need them. Keep in mind, though, that it probably will not be necessary to start at the beginning again. Instead, begin at the point that will help the older struggling reader most, based on your assessments on segmenting and blending phonemes in words. Be sure to assess as you teach so that you will know how quickly to introduce each new segmenting and blending skill.

By the beginning of first grade, most children have learned the sounds that are commonly associated with each letter of the alphabet. As they make these text (or print)-to-speech connections, and begin to use them to read and build words, they become more phonemically aware (Shaywitz, 2003). This reciprocal relationship is important; however, don't delay phonics instruction for students who have not yet acquired phonemic awareness. Teaching letter-sound correspondences along with phonemic awareness gives students opportunities to develop in both areas (Perfetti, Beck, Bell, & Hughes, 1987).

Seven Ways to Provide Practice in Segmenting and Blending Words

To prevent problems, sometimes all that is needed is additional practice. Troia, Roth, and Graham (1998) suggest the following activities, which increase in difficulty.

- **matching** (e.g., "Show me which picture rhymes with *mouse*. Which of these words begins with the same sound as *car: tooth, sock, coat?*")

- **oddity detection** (e.g., "Show me which picture does not begin with /p/. Point to the picture that does not end with the same sound as *sun*. Which of these words does not begin with the same sound as *sun: Sunday, sunshine, cowboy, sunglasses?*")

- **same/different judgment** (e.g., "Does *coat* start with the /k/ sound? When you put them together, do these sounds make the word *race*: r-a-s?")

- **segment isolation** (e.g., "What is the first sound of *chalk*? What is the first part of *sidewalk*? What is the sound at the end of *husk*?")

- **production** (e.g., "Tell me a word that begins with /s/. Tell me a word that ends with the same sound as *tap*. Tell me each sound in the word *shock*.")

- **counting** (e.g., "Count the number of parts you hear in *cage*. How many sounds are in the word *ride*?)

- **compound production** (e.g., "Tell me the word you get when you change the /p/ in *map* to /n/. Say *feel*. Now say *eel*. What sound did you leave out?")

Even with the most well-designed early instruction, evidence suggests that many learners, like Thomas, will still experience difficulties with delays in phonemic awareness development (Torgesen, Wagner, & Rashotte, 1994). For these students, more carefully designed instruction is required. The following section describes how to apply the intervention framework, introduced in Chapter 1, to phonemic awareness instruction. It includes specific strategies for developing phonemic awareness for students who are experiencing early reading difficulties, followed by a sample phonemic awareness lesson.

Applying the Intervention Framework to Phonemic Awareness

If you teach grade one or higher and your students have not acquired phonemic awareness, you need to apply the intervention framework. In this section we discuss in general terms how the framework works with phonemic awareness instruction. Later in this chapter, we present a sample lesson.

Assess and Diagnose

There are three types of tools needed to assess and diagnose phonemic awareness. *Screening tools* and *diagnostic tools* are used in Assess and Diagnose. *Progress monitoring tools* are used in Reassess.

Screening Tools

Screening tools help you decide which students need extra attention and monitoring. One kind of screening tool is observation of students, based on your understanding of how phonemic awareness develops. For example, you probably know that by midyear a typical kindergartner can segment the initial sound in a word from the remainder of a word. A first grader who can still do only that probably needs extra help.

Several formal tools are widely used to screen phonemic awareness. Your local system or state department may be able to supply you with one or even require the use of one. Figure 3.2 lists three published tools, which yield very specific information about a student's phonemic awareness.

Screening Tool	Publication Information
Comprehensive Test of Phonological Processing (CTOPP)	Pro-Ed, Austin, TX
Dynamic Indicators of Basic Early Literacy Skills: Initial Sound Fluency (6th Edition) (2003)	http://dibels.uoregon.edu University of Oregon, Eugene; SoprisWest, Longmont, CO
Texas Primary Reading Inventory	Texas Education Agency, Austin

FIGURE 3.2 Tools for screening phonemic awareness

Diagnostic Tools

While a screening tool is designed to tell you if a student is struggling or likely to struggle, a diagnostic tool is designed to tell you specifically what a student can and cannot do. When we know specific things a child can and cannot do, we can plan better, more targeted intervention. The range of tasks the test-taker is asked to do should reflect the developmental stage that a reader has achieved. For example, we know that as children develop phonological awareness, they typically understand the sound structure of words starting with larger word parts (e.g., onsets and rimes such as /th/ and /ing/ make *thing*) and then move to smaller word parts such as individual phonemes. Likewise, beginning readers are usually able to detect and segment the beginning sound of a word before the final sound or medial sounds.

The Comprehensive Test of Phonemic Processing (CTOPP; Pro-Ed), which is listed as a screening tool in Figure 3.2, provides several supplemental assessments that allow a teacher to identify a student's specific strengths and weaknesses in phonemic awareness.

You may also be able to diagnose student needs by using an informal checklist, such as the one in Figure 3.3. Figure 3.4 shows a filled-in version for Thomas, the struggling 6-year-old student described at the beginning of this chapter. Note that there are places to observe the same student on different dates, to monitor growth over time.

OBSERVATION CHECKLIST
Phonemic Awareness

+ SKILL PERFORMED CORRECTLY
- SKILL NOT PERFORMED
/ SKILL PERFORMED INACCURATELY

Name_____ Grade _____ Age _____

Phonemic Awareness Skill	Dates Observed							Comments
Rhyming/Alliteration								
Completes simple rhymes started by teacher								
Repeats alliterations with model								
Onset-Rime Blending and Segmentation								
Identifies initial sounds in spoken words								
Blends onset and rime to make a single-syllable word								
Segments a single-syllable word into its onset and rime								
Phoneme Blending and Segmentation								
Blends 3–4 phonemes to make a single-syllable word								
Segments a single-syllable word into its component phonemes								

Additional Comments:

FIGURE 3.3 Observation checklist to assess phonemic awareness

The Struggling Reader: Interventions That Work

Most likely, you will notice evidence of phonemic awareness in your students on a day-to-day basis during instructional activities, even when you are not using a checklist. Be sure to record these observations promptly because they will help you focus interventions and prevent difficulties from growing worse. If you use a checklist like the one in Figure 3.3, you may want to confirm your observations with a formal instrument.

OBSERVATION CHECKLIST

Phonemic Awareness

+ SKILL PERFORMED CORRECTLY
- SKILL NOT PERFORMED
/ SKILL PERFORMED INACCURATELY

Name __Thomas Guthrie__   Grade __K__   Age __5__

Phonemic Awareness Skill	2/4	3/10	4/13			Comments
Rhyming/Alliteration						
Completes simple rhymes started by teacher	+					2/4: Stopped testing this area after Feb.
Repeats alliterations with model	+					
Onset-Rime Blending and Segmentation						
Identifies initial sounds in spoken words	-	/	/			3/10: Inconsistently identifies initial sounds.
Blends onset and rime to make a single-syllable word	-	-				
Segments a single-syllable word into its onset and rime	-	-				
Phoneme Blending and Segmentation						
Blends 3–4 phonemes to make a single-syllable word	na	na	/			
Segments a single-syllable word into its component phonemes	na	na	/			3/10: Showing some ability here; success with "mat" and "can"

Additional Comments:

FIGURE 3.4 Sample phonemic awareness checklist filled in for Thomas

Designing Phonemic Awareness Instruction: General Guidelines

- Start with **continuous sounds** (speech sounds with uninterrupted flow of sound, such as /a/, /s/, /e/, /f/, /i/, /l/, /m/, /n/, /o/, /r/, /u/, /v/, /z/), which are easier to pronounce than **stop sounds** (speech sounds in which the air flow is stopped, such as /b/, /d/, /g/, /h/, /j/, /k/, /p/, /q/, /t/, /w/, /x/, /y/.

- Carefully model each activity as you introduce it.

- Model slow and exaggerated pronunciations of continuous sounds (e.g., "mmmmap") and **iteration** (brief, repeated pronunciations) of stop sounds (e.g., "t-t-t-top") to emphasize the individual sounds.

- Move from larger units such as syllables (/side/ /walk/) and onset-rime (/p/ /at/) to smaller units such as individual phonemes (/t/ /r/ /ee/).

- Move from easier tasks such as rhyming ("Raise your hand when I say a word that ends the same as the word *top*") to more complex tasks such as blending and segmenting ("Tell me the sounds you hear in the word *mast*").

- Use pictures or concrete objects such as building blocks or bingo chips to represent the number of segments in a word.

Teach/Reteach

Studies over the past several decades have demonstrated that phonemic awareness can be taught through brief, engaging activities that focus children's attention on manipulating sounds in words, like the ones described earlier in this chapter. However, for students who have been identified as at-risk for reading difficulties because they lack phonemic awareness, intensive, explicit instruction is required (Torgesen et al., 1994). The list on the left provides general guidelines to consider when designing or selecting activities to teach phonemic awareness skills (Chard & Dickson, 1999; Troia et al., 1998).

The steps in teaching phonemic awareness are the same as for teaching any other skill.

1. Tell students what they will learn.

2. Model the task. For example, if you are teaching how to blend an onset and rime, show students how to do it before asking them to do it themselves.

3. Gradually have students model the task. For example, have them model with you.

4. Have students model, or demonstrate, the task alone.

5. Repeat steps 2–4 with several examples of the same task.

The sample lesson in the next section shows you how to help a child who is having difficulty segmenting and blending medial and final sounds.

Practice

Students should be given the opportunity to practice a skill almost immediately after it has been taught. To monitor accuracy and provide assistance as needed, practice should always be carried out under your careful guidance. If a student makes an error, stop and model the process again and have him repeat it. Unless he is successful almost 100 percent of the time, either you need to reteach or the student needs to further develop a prior skill. For example, if a student is unable to blend onsets and rimes after you've taught him how to, reassess whether the student can segment them. That will help you determine whether to reteach blending or to go back one step and reteach segmenting.

Apply

Application takes place when a student uses a skill independently. For students who have not begun to read and write, success in practice activities is sufficient to indicate readiness for the next lessons.

If struggling readers are receiving phonemic awareness instruction along with phonics instruction, look for evidence of skill application during reading and writing activities. Students should be blending sounds as they attempt to decode unfamiliar words. They should be segmenting sounds as they attempt to spell.

Reassess

Phonemic awareness should be monitored frequently. You can do this by observing students as they read easily decodable texts to see whether they are independently using phonemic awareness skills. You may also monitor student progress periodically during a school year by using a checklist you devise or one your school recommends.

You may need to monitor the progress of struggling students as often as twice a month or even weekly. A good tool for doing that is DIBELS (see Figure 3.2), which provides alternate forms for frequent monitoring of initial-sound fluency and phonemic segmentation fluency.

Sample Lesson Using the Intervention Framework With Struggling Primary Students: Blending Phonemes

This lesson is planned for Karen, a first grader who has been found to have problems blending phonemes.

Assess and Diagnose

Karen's teacher used observation and DIBELS to determine the student's strengths and weaknesses associated with phonemic awareness. Diagnosis revealed that Karen was able to segment words into sounds but was unable to blend individual sounds into words.

Teach/Reteach

OBJECTIVE: Karen will be able to accurately blend three phonemes to make a CVC (consonant-vowel-consonant) word.

MATERIALS: bingo chips, "Say It Fast" chart (Figure 3.5)

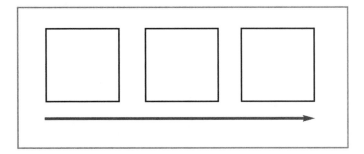

FIGURE 3.5 "Say It Fast" chart (Neuhaus Education Center, 1998)

INSTRUCTIONAL PROCEDURE: The teacher sits side-by-side with Karen, with the "Say It Fast" chart in front of them. From there, she

1. reminds Karen of her ability to segment sounds and tells her that today she will learn to blend separate sounds into words and that this will help her learn to read. She has Karen segment three CVC words with continuous consonant sounds: *sun*, *van*, and *mom*.

2. calls attention to the "Say It Fast" chart and explains that each box represents one sound. Tells Karen that she (the teacher) is going to blend three sounds to make a word and, as she says each sound, she will move a bingo chip into a box. Goes on to explain that the arrow on the chart will remind her to say the word fast after blending the three sounds.

3. models the activity by saying, "Listen as I blend sounds to make a word. I'm going to move a chip for each sound I say; each box can only have one chip."

4. says the word slowly, stretching out the sounds while sliding a chip into each box while making each sound: /mmmmaaaaaaaannnnnn/.

5. says it fast: *man*.

6. models several more examples of short CVC words using continuous sounds: *sam*, *fan*, *sis*, *mess*, *fuss*.

7. has Karen think of a word, segment it, and model blending sounds while moving chips into the boxes, and then saying the word fast.

8. continues the activity until Karen is able to segment a CVC word into separate sounds, blend the three sounds, and then say the word fast.

COMMENTS: Note that this lesson is focused just on phonemic awareness, not on letter-sound relationships. The student has already been taught to segment sounds (listen to a word and separate the sounds) and is learning to blend sounds (produce separate sounds and blend into a word). In Chapter 4, we talk about the importance of blending sounds while learning letter-sound relationships as a way to promote word-recognition skills in older children.

Practice

Have students practice segmenting and blending sounds in words using the "Say It Fast" chart. Sit with students and monitor their efforts, using your own "Say It Fast" chart. If a student isn't successful 100 percent of the time, stop and model.

Most likely, very young students to whom you teach phonemic awareness lessons have not yet been taught the letters that stand for the sounds. They won't be able to recognize a letter and make the correct sound. Therefore you must guide practice activities.

After students are successful in using the "Say It Fast" chart, try this game with small groups:

Children practice segmenting and blending phonemes as they play Beanbag Toss.

Beanbag Toss

- Have children stand in a small circle with you.
- Say a CVC (consonant-vowel-consonant) word such as *man*.
- Toss the beanbag to a child and ask him or her to segment the sounds.
- Have that child toss the beanbag to another child who blends the sounds back into the word.
- Have that child say a new word and toss the beanbag to another child who segments the word into sounds.
- Continue until everyone has had several chances.

(This game can also be played by rolling a ball while seated on the floor.)

If you are combining phonemic awareness lessons with introductory letter-recognition and phonics lessons, you might ask students to use letters as they segment and blend word sounds during the game.

Apply

Application of a phonemic awareness skill differs from practice mostly in the degree to which students carry out activities independently. When students apply skills, they should receive less assistance from you. As you observe children engaged in activities, make sure they are able to segment and blend individual sounds in words.

Of course, purposeful segmenting and blending sounds will not occur until children are beginning to work with print—in other words, when children start learning the letters of the alphabet and the sounds associated with them.

COMMENTS: There is no need to teach phonemic awareness lessons for each sound in our language, although you may want to teach lessons in words with four or five phonemes. Phonemic awareness involves the ability to hear the individual sounds in words, to segment those sounds (say the individual sounds), and to blend individual sounds into words. Once children begin to segment words successfully, they are ready to learn the letters that stand for individual sounds and to use that knowledge to begin to decode words in print.

For struggling readers beyond the first grade, you may combine phonemic awareness lessons with the lessons in letter recognition and the association of a particular sound with each letter and combination of letters. Phonics is discussed in Chapter 4.

Reassess

Your close observation during practice activities may be enough to reassure you that a student has acquired phonemic awareness. If you are uncertain, though, or if your school system requires closer monitoring, use an instrument designed for frequent progress monitoring, such as DIBELS.

Conclusion

Phonemic awareness is a necessary prerequisite to learning to read, where readers are required to see a letter (or combination of letters) and associate the expected sound with it. It is also a prerequisite to spelling, where writers say a word to themselves, hear the sounds, and associate the appropriate letters with the sounds. For struggling readers of any age, phonemic awareness and phonics may be taught concurrently. Because phonemic awareness involves learning the sounds in words, classrooms in which it is a priority will not be silent, nor should they be. Finally, we caution the reader that it is very difficult to adequately describe phonemic awareness instruction in a book. If you do not have experience and expertise with this topic, we encourage you to seek professional development and classroom assistance while working with struggling learners.

CHAPTER 4

Word Recognition

CASE STUDY

While most of Marsha Hudson's third-grade class is reading fluently, a few of her students are still struggling to recognize words, and she is concerned about them.

In a small-group meeting, Marsha tells two students to say some words with the long-*i* sound. The students say a few words such as *bite* and *try*. She then tells them to continue to think of long-*i* words, build the words using the letter tiles, and then write them down on paper.

Madison seems to be struggling. She builds only words that end in vowel-consonant-*e* (VCe), such as *hide*. Ms. Hudson reminds her that the class has had lessons in other spellings for the long-*i* sound, but Madison just looks puzzled. Even when Ms. Hudson reminds her of the word *night*, which she read in a story, Madison is unable to spell it.

Using Madison's letter tiles, Ms. Hudson forms the word *fight* and asks Madison to read it. Madison is unable to do so. When Ms. Hudson substitutes different beginning letters to form *tight*, *night*, and *might*, Madison cannot read them. Then Ms. Hudson forms *try*, and Madison cannot read that word either.

According to Ms. Hudson, Madison has been taught ways to decode both kinds of long-*i* words—those ending in *-ight* and those ending in *y*. Still, Madison struggles to read words containing those patterns, whether in isolation or in connected text.

Like Madison, many students experience difficulties with skills related to word recognition. In fact, it is one of the most common problems for students identified as having severe reading difficulties (Shaywitz, 2003; Stanovich, 1986). We begin this chapter with a discussion of what word recognition is and why it is important. Then we explain how children develop word recognition and present guidelines for good initial teaching of word-recognition skills. From there, we explain how to apply the intervention framework to teaching (or reteaching) word-recognition skills to struggling readers, showing how that teaching changes depending on the words or word parts. Finally, we present a sample intervention lesson for a specific word-recognition skill.

What Is Word Recognition?

Word recognition is the ability to read words, an act that sounds deceptively simple. Unfortunately, it's *not* simple. The fact that many people read words with ease sometimes causes us to assume the skill develops naturally without direct instruction, as speech does for most children. However, word recognition must be taught. Specifically, children must be shown how to carry out two very important and complex processes:

1. Looking at letters or letter combinations of the word, identifying the sounds that correspond to those letters or letter combinations, and blending the sounds together to pronounce the word.

2. Matching the pronunciation of the blended sounds with a word that the learner already knows—that is, a word in his or her oral language.

So, strong word recognition depends on the reader being able to get the correct pronunciation of the word (or a close approximation) and having the vocabulary knowledge to make sense of it.

In this chapter, we focus on the first process. In Chapter 5, we discuss how to increase students' vocabularies so they are better able to make sense of the words they read.

Why Is Word Recognition So Important?

Word recognition is important because without it readers cannot access the meaning of an author's message. Comprehension depends on the reader's ability to decode the words selected by the author to convey the message (National Research Council, 1998). As children become successful in word recognition, their vocabulary grows and their content knowledge becomes more sophisticated (Cunningham & Stanovich, 1998). In fact, beyond second grade, reading is a primary way students gain new vocabulary, and it plays a major role in content area learning. Therefore, students must become proficient at word recognition.

Students gain proficiency by applying a reliable, step-by-step strategy for recognizing familiar words and figuring out unfamiliar words (Chard & Osborn, 1999). Readers who have such a strategy are able to read a wide range of print and electronic text. Whether they are reading a surfing magazine, a fantasy book, or dinosaur cards, they are rewarded by their ability to understand the text and by a desire to read more. In short, when readers have a strategy for word recognition, they enjoy reading and read more. When they read more, they become better readers (Cunningham & Stanovich, 1998).

The consequences of not being able to recognize words can be devastating. Cunningham and Stanovich (1998) argue that poor word readers do not find reading rewarding and, consequently, do not read enough to learn new words and practice familiar words. As a result, they do not develop strong vocabularies and are not able to understand what they read, unlike students who read a lot (Stanovich, 1986).

Like any single aspect of reading, word recognition is necessary but not sufficient for understanding texts and ensuring proficient reading. But the fact remains, if students struggle with word recognition they are unlikely to understand what an author is trying to communicate. In fact, for struggling readers, it is often a primary barrier to reading proficiency (Chard, Simmons, & Kame'enui, 1998; Stanovich, 1986). In order to help struggling readers overcome this barrier, it is critical to know how word recognition develops.

How Do Students Develop Word Recognition?

Before children can learn to read words well, they must meet four prerequisite conditions (Chard et al., 1998):

Recognize the Purposes of Print

Texts are created for a reason, whether it is to entertain, inform, direct, or persuade, and young children need to be made aware of that. From early on, many children observe parents and siblings using text to communicate with others (e.g., letters, notes on the fridge, messages in the lunch box, greeting cards) or with themselves (e.g., grocery lists, reminder notes, to-do lists, recipes). For most children, building this awareness does not require explicit instruction. Parents simply need to make sure their children see them using text to communicate.

Recognize the Letters of the Alphabet

One reason that reading is far less natural than speech is that it depends on the use of letters. Being able to name the letters of the alphabet accurately and quickly is a strong predictor of later success in reading. Letter recognition is important to reading for many reasons (Adams, 1990). Most importantly, perhaps, letter recognition makes it easier to focus on learning the sounds and spelling patterns of words. That said, students need not master the names of all the letters of the alphabet before you begin word-recognition instruction. With just a few consonants and a vowel, children can begin to read and write short words.

Students must also understand the alphabetic principle, the fact that words are made up of letters that represent sounds. We discuss this concept in the next section.

Understand That Print Represents Speech

We often take the print around us for granted. Yet, to children, print in the environment can go unnoticed or remain mysterious if no one points out that it can be spoken. As with recognizing the purposes of print, this understanding can be developed very early with only a little attention. Encourage parents of preschoolers to demonstrate how the print on objects such as cereal boxes, soup cans, road signs, books, and newspapers stands for words that can be said aloud.

This will send a strong message that print not only has meaning, but also that it has a purpose.

Acquire Phonemic Awareness

Frequently, children who are not successful word readers in first grade lack phonemic awareness (Juel, Griffith, & Gough, 1986). A significant amount of research conducted on phonemic awareness over the past several decades points to this fact. For students who are struggling with phonemic awareness, try the intervention ideas in Chapter 3.

For some children, these conditions are sufficient for them to begin reading words spontaneously. However, for many children, they are not enough. Reading continues to be a struggle. Meeting the needs of those struggling readers is the focus of this chapter.

Word recognition requires that children grasp the alphabetic principle. That is, they need to understand that words are made up of letters that represent sounds and that knowing the relationship between letters and sounds will help them read unfamiliar words. The ability to acquire the alphabetic principle and apply it to word recognition develops as children learn about how letters, sounds, and words work. To understand this development, it's useful to look at Ehri's (1998) stages: pre-alphabetic, partial alphabetic, fully alphabetic, and consolidated alphabetic. Figure 4.1 describes each stage and identifies the approximate age and grade level at which children typically reach a given stage. The final column lists implications of each stage for teaching.

How Do Students Learn to Recognize Words?

Ehri's stages help us understand that there is a cohesive sequence to word-recognition development and that struggling readers may have trouble because they have not received instruction that reflects that sequence. Without that instruction, struggling readers often become too dependent on context or pictures to recognize new words quickly and accurately (Adams, 1990; Stanovich, 1980). Developing readers need to be taught to be flexible and strategic in their approach to identifying words. Initially, they need to rely on decoding words sequentially, by attending to the sounds and letters in them and monitoring their level of success to make sure they understand what they're reading (Learning

Stage of Reading Development	Description of Student Knowledge	Typical Age/ Grade Level	Implications for Teaching
Pre-alphabetic	Students have little or no understanding of the alphabetic principle; children may recognize words by the shape of their first letter (e.g., McDonalds is recognized by the shape of the M of the golden arches).	3–6 years/ Pre K–K	• Be sure children meet the prerequisite conditions for word recognition listed on pages 53–54. • Begin teaching common letter-sound relationships.
Partial Alphabetic	Students have an initial grasp of the connection between letters and sounds and can take advantage of these connections to read simple words (e.g., can recognize the word *cat* because of the /c/ sound at the beginning and the /t/ sound at the end).	5–8 years/K–1	Teach children: • all common **letter-sound relationships**, • to blend **regular words**, • irregular word recognition, • to read simple stories using readable texts, and • a generalizable strategy for word recognition that can be used with unfamiliar words.
Fully Alphabetic	Students are familiar with most letter-sound relationships and can use their knowledge of blending to read unfamiliar words; many familiar words become instantly recognizable after several exposures.	6–8 years/ Late K–2	• Reinforce common letter-sound relationships, simple word structures, and **irregular words** through assisted reading. • Encourage automatic word recognition. • Begin teaching advanced word analysis. • Reinforce word-recognition strategy.
Consolidated Alphabetic	Students begin to economize by recognizing word chunks (e.g., -*ight*) and using these patterns to read unfamiliar words more quickly.	7 years– adulthood/ 2 and beyond	• Teach children more advanced word-analysis skills. • Reinforce word-recognition strategy.

FIGURE 4.1 Practical implications of Ehri's stages of reading development

First Alliance, 1998; National Reading Panel, 2000). As their experience with text grows, they will recognize clusters of letters and whole words, and become fluent readers (Chard & Osborn, 1999). For struggling readers, a systematic and explicit approach to word-recognition instruction is particularly critical (Anderson, Heibert, Scott, & Wilkinson, 1985).

A system for teaching word recognition that reflects Ehri's stages is described below. If you use this system for all students in the early primary grades, you will likely prevent many of them from experiencing long-term difficulties with word recognition. The system is made up of five elements: letter-sound relationships, regular-word recognition (words that are spelled as they sound), irregular-word recognition (words that are spelled differently from the way they sound), advanced word analysis, and story reading. Mastery of each of these elements contributes to the development of a word-recognition strategy. For example, when students master letter-sound relationships, they are likely to be able to read regular words. Below, we describe each element and general guidelines for teaching it.

Continuous Sounds		Stop Sounds	
a	fat	b	boy
e	set	c	cat
f	fit	d	dad
i	sit	g	get
l	left	h	ham
m	mat	j	jug
n	not	k	kick
o	lot	p	pit
r	ran	q	quit
s	send	t	tap
u	cut	x	fox
v	vat		
w	well		
y	yes		
z	zoom		

FIGURE 4.2 Common sound-spellings of single letters (Source: Carnine, Silbert, Kame'enui, & Tarver, 2004)

Letter-Sound Relationships

To begin decoding words, children need to be able to recognize the sounds that are associated with individual letters and combinations of letters. For example, to read the word *sit*, a reader needs to know the sounds for *s*, *i*, and *t*. Most children learn the most common letter-sound relationships easily. However, struggling readers may have trouble hearing the sounds associated with particular letters and distinguishing them from one another. Therefore, teachers working with struggling readers must know and be able to pronounce the sounds that are most commonly associated with letters and combinations of letters. See Figure 4.2 for a list of letters, their most common sounds, and a

The Struggling Reader: Interventions That Work

guide word to help you with the pronunciation of that sound. The list is divided into continuous sounds, those that can be said for several seconds without distorting them (e.g., /m/ and /s/), and stop sounds, those that become distorted if said for more than a second (e.g., /t/ and /p/). The importance of these categories will be discussed later.

When teaching letter-sound relationships, the following guidelines may be useful:

- **Teach more useful letter-sound relationships first.** The first texts you give children to read are likely to contain mostly words made up of common letters and their most common sounds such as *m, s, c,* and *t.* It is better to teach these first and then move to the less common relationships such as *x, qu,* and *z.*

- **Separate letter-sound relationships that are potentially confusing.** Many children struggle to hear the subtle distinctions between sounds such as *f* and *v,* or see the difference between letters such as *b* and *d.* You can reduce confusion by first teaching one letter in a potentially confusing pair, followed by other sounds and letters, followed by the second letter in the pair. For example, *m* and *n* look and sound alike, making them particularly challenging. So teach *m* thoroughly, then other letters that don't resemble *m* or *n* in any way, then *n.* We also recommend separating the short sounds of /a/, /e/, and /i/ in this way. Giving children several days of practice with each of these sounds individually before teaching the next will make it easier for them to learn them all. You may wonder whether it makes more sense to teach the short vowels or long vowels first. We are not aware of any research that supports one approach over the other. Rather, we think you should make this decision based on logic about what makes up words. Words are composed of vowels and consonants. Therefore, it is most useful for students to learn enough vowels and consonants to be able to read some words. If a struggling reader has particular problems in a given area, then you should focus your instruction around the student's needs.

A student is taught to blend sounds together silently.

- **Teach continuous sounds before stop sounds.** Children often find it easier to pronounce continuous sounds, sounds such as /m/ and /s/ that can be said for a few seconds without changing to a different sound. (Try pronouncing /m/. Even after a few seconds it still sounds like the sound of *m*.) However, the stop sounds can't be said for several seconds because the sound changes. It is not possible to teach all continuous sounds before stop sounds because not many words could be made. However, we suggest teaching several continuous sounds first to get children started.

- **Pace letter-sound instruction based on student success.** Begin by teaching two letter-sound relationships per week. Carefully monitor student success by calling on individual students to identify the sounds of letters. If students can't do what you're asking, your rate of introduction is too fast. Once students have mastered a few letter-sound relationships, teach them to build words such as *mat* and *sat*, and to read simple sentences. This direct application provides a review of letter-sound relationships and reinforces the purpose of learning phonics.

Regular-Word Recognition

Regular words are words made up of letters that represent their most common sounds. For example, *sad* is a regular word because all of the letters stand for their common sounds; *said* is not, because the vowel digraph, *ai*, has a short-*e* sound. See Figure 4.2 for more examples of regular words. Starting instruction with regular words allows students to apply the letter-sound relationships they have been taught. For struggling readers, it is important to focus first on regular words that include sounds that they have mastered, which increases their chances of reading the words correctly (Carnine et al., 2004). Teach students to follow this three-step process to build regular-word recognition skills:

Step 1: Sound out the word. Students produce each letter sound in sequence, from left to right. In other words, they sound out the word. We recommend having students slowly blend the sounds together, trying not to stop between them, which helps them determine whether they are pronouncing the word correctly.

Step 2: Say the word quickly. Once students can blend each sound without stopping, show them how to run the sounds together to sound like a word.

Step 3: Sound out the word in your head before reading it aloud. When students are able to sound out words and say them fast, tell them to do Step 1 in their heads before saying the whole word aloud. Model this step by silently mouthing the sounds of the word before saying the word. It is important for students to practice sounding out words silently to facilitate their automatic word recognition and to teach them how it feels to read silently like proficient readers.

Teaching Regular-Word Recognition: More Guidelines

- Teach sounding-out initially with words that contain only continuous sounds (or stop sounds only in the final position, e.g., *am*, *sam*, *man*, *sat*, *mop*, *sit*).

- During initial instruction, choose words that progress from short vowel-consonant words (e.g., *it*, *an*, *at*) to consonant-vowel-consonant words (e.g., *mit*, *fan*, *cat*) that contain letters representing their most common sounds. Incorporate more complex spelling patterns (e.g., CVCC, CCVC) as students demonstrate proficiency in simple word recognition.

- Use words that are in children's oral language, such as words for simple concepts and actions (e.g., *kid*, *cat*, *pig*, *big*, *nap*, *run*). Early word recognition is a complex process for struggling readers. Their efforts to read a word should result in a word that is meaningful to them.

Irregular-Word Recognition

Some common words that occur frequently in text, such as *the*, *said*, and *because*, do not conform to the usual sound-letter relationships. Therefore, students cannot sound them out. Instead, they need to learn these words by paying attention to their unique spellings and pronunciations. Here are some ways to help them do that:

- Teach the most useful words first, meaning those that appear often in stories and informational books. Consider following common high-frequency word lists such as The Fry Instant Word List, the 227 Core Words Derived from 400 Storybooks for Beginning Readers, or the Dolch Basic Sight Vocabulary. Copies of these lists can be found in *Literacy Assessment: Helping Teachers Plan Instruction*, Second Edition, Cooper and Kiger, 2005.

- Monitor success as you teach and as students practice new words. We recommend that you start by introducing three to five high-frequency words at a time. If students struggle, limit the number of words introduced in a lesson to one or two.

- Include frequent, but brief, opportunities for children to practice reading irregular word lists until they recognize each word automatically. Lists used for practice should contain no more than six to ten words.

- If possible, teach irregular words for about five minutes per day for one or two days before expecting students to read them in texts. This gives students ample time to practice the words so that they will recognize them in context.

Advanced Word Recognition

By learning to recognize "larger chunks" in words, students grow more efficient in their word recognition. These "larger chunks" fall into four categories: blends, letter combinations, vowel-consonant-*e* patterns, and **affixes**:

Blends are strings of consonants that make their common sounds such that each sound can be heard in the word (e.g. *-st*, *spl-*).

Letter Combinations describes a wide range of spelling patterns that include **consonant digraphs** (combinations of consonants that make a single sound, e.g., *sh, ph, wh, ng*), **vowel digraphs** (vowel pairs that make a single sound, e.g., *ai, ee, oa, ie*), **diphthong** (a blend of vowel sounds in one syllable, e.g., *oi, oy, ow*), and **r-controlled vowels** (vowels that when combined with *-r* change their sound, e.g., *ar, ir, ur*).

Vowel-Consonant-e Patterns include words in which a consonant separates any vowel from a silent *e*, resulting in the preceding vowel saying its name (e.g., *kite, rode, lake*).

Affixes are word parts such as prefixes, suffixes, and inflectional endings that are commonly added to the beginning or ending of a word to change its meaning (e.g., *pre-, epi-, -ment, -ed*).

The following guidelines will help you make decisions about the pace and sequence of your advanced word-recognition instruction:

- As with letter-sound relationships, we recommend introducing more common letter combinations (e.g., consonant digraph *sh*) before less common combinations (e.g., consonant digraph *ph*). This will help children read and write words that appear in the text they are reading.

- Attempt to separate lessons in word parts that are easily confused because they look similar (e.g., *was* and *saw*; *of* and *off*) or sound similar (e.g., words with *r*-controlled vowels, such as *star* and *stir*).

- Once children know short and long vowel sounds, teach the vowel-consonant-*e* pattern (VCe) and have them begin to practice reading words that contain that pattern, as well as making discriminations between CVC words and VCe words such as *hop/hope* and *pin/pine*.

- For younger struggling readers, introduce only affixes that are common in early literature (e.g., *re-, un-, dis-, con-, -ness, -ful,* and *-ion*). As students learn more about how words and word parts interact to change meaning, introduce more sophisticated affixes.

Story Reading

Struggling readers should have many opportunities to apply their newly learned decoding strategies in connected text. The following guidelines are likely to help them do that while reading stories:

- Select stories that contain a high percentage of words that correspond to the letter-sound relationships that you have taught (Beck, 1998; Juel & Roper-Schneider, 1985; Stanovich, 1991). These are called decodable books. Nearly all publishers of reading materials produce sets of these books.

- Provide students with opportunities to reread familiar stories to build accuracy in word recognition and fluency with connected texts.

- Praise students whenever they use the sounding-out strategy aloud, while gently challenging them to move to sounding out words in their head.

- Gradually increase the difficulty of the stories by continuously introducing ones that contain new phonic elements, high-frequency words, and irregular words as these are taught.

Converging evidence suggests that word recognition begins with a strong command of the alphabetic principle and the ability to blend sounds to make words (Stanovich, 1991). Once this skill is mastered and performed in connected text, knowledge of sentence structure, vocabulary, and context helps the reader move fluently through the text and make sense of the author's message.

Knowing how word recognition develops gives us the background we need to design appropriate intervention. Too often, children who are struggling with word recognition receive interventions that focus on using syntax and context when they really only need to overcome the challenge of using their knowledge of letters and sounds to pronounce the words. The consequence of ignoring the primary importance of sounding out words is that struggling readers fail to master decoding and are unable to read proficiently.

Proficient readers, including fluent adult readers, process virtually every word as they read (Rayner & Pollatsek, 1989). If this is the case, why do good readers seem to do it so effortlessly? The answer is practice. Learning to read words is only one step to fluent reading. In Chapter 6, we will discuss how to help readers who are having difficulty with fluency.

The guidelines we have outlined here will help you prevent word-recognition difficulties for most of your students. However, even with these guidelines, you will most likely have students who need more strategic instruction that is based on their specific needs. The following section focuses on how to apply the intervention framework to help struggling readers with word-recognition difficulties. From there, we present a complete sample lesson on one particular word-recognition skill, r-controlled vowels.

Applying the Intervention Framework to Word Recognition

In Chapter 1 we introduced you to an intervention framework that included five steps: (1) assess and diagnose, (2) teach/reteach, (3) practice, (4) apply, and (5) reassess. Here, each of these steps is described in the context of word-recognition instruction.

Assess and Diagnose

Screen To diagnose your students accurately and decide who might be at risk for difficulties in reading words, start screening them toward the end of first grade. One of the most effective ways to do that is by asking students to read a list of nonsense (or pseudo) words. Students are asked to read a list of letter strings that look like conventional words, such as *som* or *vit*. The purpose of using nonsense words is to determine whether the reader can apply a decoding strategy when there is no support provided from context or word familiarity.

Dynamic Indicators of Basic Early Literacy Skills - Nonsense Word Fluency (*DIBELS-NWF*) (Good & Kaminski, 2002), a good example of a published tool, is designed to help you determine which students are likely to need additional support or intervention in decoding. Students are given one minute to read a list of single-syllable nonsense words or to identify the **letter-sound correspondences** that make up the nonsense words (See Figure 4.3 for an example). DIBELS-NWF is part of a system of measures that are available for free download at http://dibels. uoregon.edu. Scoring procedures and benchmark scores are also available at this Web site.

Some teachers are loath to use nonsense words because students expect words to have meaning and, therefore, try to force nonsense words into being "real"

kik	woj	sig	faj	yis
kaj	fek	av	zin	zez
lan	nul	zem	og	nom
yuf	pos	vok	viv	feg
bub	dij	sij	vus	tos
wuv	nij	pik	nok	mot
nif	vec	al	boj	nen
suv	yig	dit	tum	joj
yaf	zof	um	vim	vel
tig	mak	sog	wot	sav

FIGURE 4.3 Example of nonsense word fluency measure (Kaminski & Good, 1996)

words. If this happens, stop the test and take a few minutes to explain the concept before proceeding.

Diagnosis After screening, you may need more detailed diagnostic information to help you plan instruction for some students. There are many tests designed to help you target students' needs more precisely. Most include many of the same components, among them:

- matching sounds corresponding to a sequence of letters.

- reading a series of increasingly difficult regular words.

- reading a series of increasingly difficult irregular words.

- reading connected text passages.

Based on how well the student carries out these activities, you will be able to tell which skill areas give him or her the most trouble.

Basic Phonics Skills Test (BPST) (Shefelbine, 1996), an example of a diagnostic test for word recognition, is commonly used to determine students' phonics and word-recognition skills and to help teachers make decisions about where to begin instruction. You can also use components of published reading tests, such as the *Woodcock Reading Mastery Test-Revised* (Woodcock, 2000), which includes sections on phonics and decoding. If you prefer to develop your own diagnostic measure for word recognition, consider using a resource such as *Direct Instruction Reading* (Carnine et al., 2004) to assist you in making decisions about how to structure the test and what to include.

Too often teachers spend a great deal of time developing and administering diagnostic measures for word recognition but do not use the results to guide instructional decisions. So, whether you are planning to use published or self-created measures, be sure to use your findings to inform your instruction. Otherwise, why assess students in the first place?

Teach/Reteach

Once you determine a student's need, the next step is to teach the skill to address that need. If the student is like most struggling readers, he or she has been taught the skill in the past but did not learn it. Therefore, your instruction must be explicit and clear. Here are examples of initial teaching for four of the five elements of word recognition: letter-sound knowledge, regular-word reading, irregular-word reading, and advanced word analysis.

Initial Instruction in Letter-Sound Knowledge

This is how you might teach students the sound associated with the double-*e* spelling pattern in words such as *eel, sheep,* and *knee.*

TARGET SKILL: long-*e* sound (*ee*)

Place a letter combination card (e.g., *ee*) on the chalk tray or a desktop. Point at the card.

TEACHER:	These letters say /ē/ (long e). Listen again: /ē/ (long e). [*Say the sound for one or two seconds while pointing.*] Now it is your turn. When I point to the letters, you say the sound. Remember to say the sound for as long as I'm pointing.
STUDENT(S):	/ē/
TEACHER:	Excellent. That is /ē/. [*If there are two or more students in the group, randomly call on individuals to say the sound. Continue by providing word cards that contain the target sound/letter and follow the same procedure.*]

Initial Instruction in Regular-Word Recognition

Below is an example of how you might teach children to blend sounds to read a word.

TARGET SKILL: CVC word recognition

Place letter cards or a word card for the target word (e.g., *sit*) in the chalk tray or write the word clearly on a white board.

TEACHER: We have learned all the sounds in this word. Watch carefully as I show you how to sound it out and read the whole word. [*Move your finger under each letter as you say its sound, without stopping between the sounds.*]

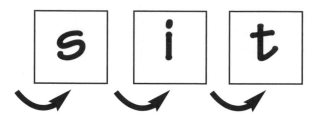

sssssssiiiiiiiiiit. sit. The word is sit. [*Repeat.*] Now it is your turn. Say the sounds as I touch each letter. When you are finished, say the whole word. [*Move your finger under each letter as students say the sounds. Remind students not to stop between sounds.*]

STUDENT(S): sssssssiiiiiiiit

TEACHER: Say the whole word.

STUDENT(S): sit

[*If there are two or more students in the group, randomly select students to sound out and read* sit *individually.*]

For some struggling readers, you may need to use concrete objects such as letter tiles to support their blending initially. For example, when helping a student blend /s/ /i/ /t/, you might have her point to, identify, and sound out the letters separately. Next, have her move the letters closer together and blend the sounds. Finally, have her move the letters so that they're touching and blend the sounds more quickly. Moving concrete representations of the letter-sound connections together provides a scaffold for many learners to blend the sounds without stopping.

Initial Instruction in Irregular-Word Recognition

Here is an example of how you might teach an irregular word.

TARGET SKILL: Reading the word *because*

Place a word card that reads *because* in the chalk tray or write the word clearly on a white board.

TEACHER: This is a word that doesn't sound exactly the way it looks. The word is *because*. [*Point to the word.*] Say it with me.

TEACHER/STUDENT(S): because

TEACHER: Your turn. Say the word as I point to it.

STUDENT(S): because

[*Repeat a few times.*]

TEACHER: If you see this word in a sentence and can't remember it, try sounding out the first few letters and think about the sentence you are reading. This may help you to remember it.

Though it may seem counterintuitive to have children sound out words that do not conform to the common phonics rules, it often helps them approximate the word while also using contextual analysis and their understanding of syntax (Ehri, 1998).

Initial Instruction in Advanced Word Recognition

Below is an example of how you might teach an advanced word-recognition skill.

TARGET SKILL: Reading words with vowel-consonant-*e* spelling pattern, such as *cane* and *dime*

Write the word *kit* on the white board.

TEACHER: Here is a word we all know how to read. Everyone read it with me.

TEACHER/STUDENT(S): kit

TEACHER: I'm going to add an e at the end of this word. When you see a word with a vowel, a consonant, and an e, the e is silent and the vowel will usually say its name. So, this word is now *kite*. Read it with me.

TEACHER/STUDENT(S): kite

TEACHER: That's right, it is *kite*. Notice how the sound of the *i* changes when we add an e—from short *i* to long *i*, in other words to an *i* that says its name. I'm going to show you another word with the vowel-consonant-e pattern. [*Write the word* pan *on the white board.*]

TEACHER: Everyone, what is this word?

STUDENT(S): pan

TEACHER: That's right, it is *pan*. Now, when I add an e, it now has a vowel-consonant-e pattern and the *a* says its name. The word is *pane*. Read it with me.

TEACHER/STUDENT(S): pane

Practice

The example lessons for teaching the elements of word recognition are brief for good reason: If we dwell on isolated phonic elements or irregular words for too long, children come to believe that reading is not very meaningful. This is true of word-recognition practice activities as well. Effective practice should help students build mastery so that they can use these skills spontaneously, with little or no attention to isolated parts—in other words, with automaticity—as they read connected text. Here are examples of three good practice activities, followed by guidelines for creating others.

Practicing Letter-Sound Correspondences: Letter Race This activity builds students' automaticity with previously taught letter-sound correspondences. Group the class into partners. Give each pair of students about ten cards containing individual letters that they know and whose sounds are familiar to them. Set a timer for one minute. Have one student hold up cards one at a time while the partner tells the sound that corresponds to the letter. If a student misses a letter and the partner catches the error, direct the partner to put that word back in the deck so that the student who missed it has a chance to try it again. When the bell rings, ask partners to change roles. Since this activity takes no more than three minutes, it can be done multiple times in a day.

Practicing Regular and Irregular Words: 5-by-5 Grid This activity is designed to give students lots of practice with reading words they have been taught. Arrange five words in a 5-by-5 grid, as in the illustration below. The grid can be made using word cards on a table or by writing words in a template.

ship	trap	have	trap	past
have	like	trap	ship	like
trap	have	ship	like	have
past	ship	past	past	trap
like	past	like	have	ship

Direct students, either individually or in pairs, to read as many words as possible down the columns or across the rows in one minute. If a student makes an error, you or the partner can correct her and have her read that row or column again.

Practice Reading Words: Personal Word Walls Help each of your students create a personal word wall to give them practice in recognizing words and building automaticity several times a day. Divide the inside of a file folder into sections corresponding to the letters of the alphabet or other spelling pattern (e.g., *sh* or *ing*). As students learn to read new words, have them write those words on masking tape and affix them inside the file folder, under the corresponding letter or spelling pattern. Periodically throughout the day, have students take out their "word wall" folders and practice reading the words. Once they demonstrate mastery of a word (meaning they can read it accurately in one to two seconds) have them remove the word, take it home to show their family, and replace it with another word. This gives students a sense of accomplishment as their list of mastered words grows.

Apply

In their 1985 landmark report on reading instruction, *Becoming a Nation of Readers*, Anderson et al. (1985) stated that "the best way to get children to refine and extend their knowledge of letter-sound correspondences is through *repeated opportunities to read*" (p. 38). We agree. This is where the fifth element, story reading, comes into play. Keep in mind, though, with students experiencing difficulty with word recognition, that book selection is particularly important. While we often feel a sense of urgency to get students reading authentic children's literature, we recommend using text that is

Developing Practice Activities for Word Recognition: General Guidelines

Activities should:

- be brief, no more than three minutes

- focus on learned phonic elements, spelling patterns, or words students need in order to build automaticity

- be designed to engage as many students as possible simultaneously (e.g., partner-based or individual practice)

- include only five to ten letters or words to ensure that students get multiple exposures to them

accessible based on the skills the child has mastered prior to reading. Here are a few guidelines to follow when selecting appropriate texts:

- Ensure that the phonic elements, high-frequency words, and irregular words in the text have been mastered by the student.

- Prior to the first reading, isolate phonic elements and words that may be barriers to the student's success and have the student read them so that she has a better chance of recognizing them in continuous text.

- Provide the student with ample opportunity to read and reread stories and expository texts to build confidence and fluency.

- Systematically increase the difficulty of texts as the student masters more phonic elements and words.

If you follow these guidelines, your students should be able to read less-controlled, more-authentic children's literature after just a few months. That said, students should have access to good literature during the day for purposes other than instruction in word recognition. For example, during teacher Read Alouds, library visits, and content area instruction, students who are struggling with independent reading can be and should be exposed to literature that they may not yet be able to read on their own.

Reassess

Because developing word recognition is so important for students who have a history of problems with reading, we must be sure they are making continuous progress as we provide intervention. There are formal and informal ways to do that. Here are two examples:

Formal Progress Monitoring The *DIBELS Nonsense Word Fluency* (NWF) measure (Kaminski & Good, 1996; Good & Kaminski, 2002) that we described earlier in this chapter can provide you with the evidence you need. If students are truly learning phonic elements and early word blending, you will see steady growth in their NWF scores. If a student does not appear to be making progress within two to three weeks despite targeted intervention, this is a signal that your instruction is not working and needs to be modified.

Informal Progress Monitoring In addition to monitoring students' progress with the DIBELS-NWF, use informal assessments such as a checklist to gauge students' word growth as they read letter cards, word lists, and decodable books, as well as when they're writing. Figure 4.4 presents a form for monitoring progress. As you teach, note when a student demonstrates knowledge of a particular sound or letter combination. Each numbered word is keyed to a specific skill. For example, if a child can read #83, *enjoyable*, it is safe to assume that she recognizes the word part *able*. You might also create a student copy of just the key words that contain parts that have been taught and informally assess by asking her to read those words aloud.

The point at which a student begins to struggle gives you a sense of where to begin instruction. For example, if the student is unable to read #54, *cart*, an intervention lesson on the *r*-controlled vowel *a* may help him. In the next section, we describe just such a lesson.

Sample Word-Recognition Intervention Lesson

This sample lesson is planned for Riley, a second grader who has demonstrated difficulties reading words with *r*-controlled vowels.

Assess and Diagnose

Riley's teacher suspected problems with word recognition by observing him read and write. Her suspicion was confirmed using the *Basic Phonics Skills Test* (Shefelbine, 1996). Diagnosis revealed that Riley was able to read many short words containing letters that represent their common sounds but was unable to read words with *r*-controlled vowels, such as *smart*, *stir*, and *corn*. The first lesson focuses on just one *r*-controlled vowel—the *ar* combination.

Word Recognition Monitoring Form

Name_____ Grade _____ Age _____

#	Item	Response	#	Item	Response	#	Item	Response
SOUNDS			**WORDS**			**WORDS**		
1	A		35	flag		69	taped	
2	M		36	drop		70	hoping	
3	T		37	stamp		71	timer	
4	S		38	strap		72	knock	
5	I		39	split		73	boil	
6	f		40	skunk		74	enjoy	
7	d		**Advanced Word Analysis**			75	stew	
8	r		41	bath		76	graph	
9	o		42	hunter		77	wrap	
10	g		43	testing		78	haunt	
11	l		44	shop		79	hawk	
12	h		45	landed		80	confuse	
13	u		46	licked		81	payment	
14	c		47	missed		82	distant	
15	b		48	when		83	enjoyable	
16	n		49	quiz		84	useless	
17	k		50	fold		85	darkness	
18	e		51	sunny		86	protect	
19	v		52	fastest		87	invention	
20	p		53	loan		88	sensible	
21	y		54	cart		89	package	
22	j		55	fine		90	mission	
23	x		56	hope		91	silence	
24	w		57	cane		92	selfish	
25	q		58	neat		93	predict	
26	z		59	hoop		94	compare	
Regular Words			60	candle		95	million	
27	it		61	meet		96	venture	
28	am		62	pain		97	detective	
29	mad		63	lunch		98	accuse	
30	him		64	port		99	joyous	
31	must		65	pray		100	panic	
32	flag		66	proud		101	forward	
33	trip		67	thirst		102	realize	
34	hand		68	curb		103	artist	

FIGURE 4.4 Sample monitoring form for word-recognition skills
(Adapted from Carnine et al., 2004)

Teach/Reteach

OBJECTIVE: Riley will be able to identify the r-controlled vowel *ar* and read it in one-syllable words.

MATERIALS: a card with the letters *ar* and a picture of a car, white board, dry-erase marker.

INSTRUCTIONAL PROCEDURE:

1. Sit across from Riley, near the white board.
2. Tell Riley that today you will help him learn a new sound that says /ar/. Have him warm up by reading some words that he knows (e.g., *cat, pit, bean*).
3. Call attention to the "ar" card. Point to the picture of the car and ask Riley to identify it.
4. Model pronouncing the target sound. Say: "Listen as I say this sound. This says /ar/." Repeat.
5. Pronounce the sound together. Say: "Riley, say the sound with me. /ar/." Monitor to ensure he is saying /ar/ correctly.
6. Give the student a chance to try it on his own. Say: "Now it's your turn. When I point to the letters, you say the sound." Monitor.
7. Write the word *car* on the white board. Underline the *ar* in the word.
8. Ask the student to read the word part. Say: "Riley, read the underlined word part in this word." Monitor.
9. Blend the sounds together to read *car*. Say: "Good, now listen to me read the word."
10. Say the word quickly and connect word and picture: "Car. Hey, that's the picture on my 'ar' card."
11. Give the student a try. Say: "Riley, it's your turn to read this word." Point to *car* and monitor as he reads the word.
12. Write several "ar" words on the white board (e.g., *star, far, cart, barn, part*). Have Riley sound out and read each word quickly. If he is not successful 100 percent of the time, stop and model again.

A student practices reading a list of words
with an *r*-controlled vowel pattern.

Practice

Provide practice by having Riley read short word lists and sentences that include
the target letters or letter combinations. For example:

> Sam parks her car too far from the start.

Ask Riley to underline the *ar* parts and then read the sentence, monitoring
to make sure he can identify *ar* in each word quickly and read the sentence.
Doing this activity using a few more sentences with *ar* words will serve as good
practice and build Riley's confidence.

Apply

Identify a short story or informational book that Riley can read containing several
ar words. Ask him to read the book to you to determine if he can read words
with the target letter combination. You could also ask him to read the book with
a partner and observe whether he is successful.

COMMENTS: The key to application is to give the student lots of opportunities to read the target letter or letter combination, in this case *ar*, in sentences, so that he can generalize their new skill to read more extended connected texts. Be aware, though, that many struggling readers will still need coaching before and during their reading of extended text. For example, Riley's teacher may ask him to preview a book and identify all the *ar* words before he reads it. Also, she may select one or two sentences from the text for him to read before he tries reading the whole book. This will build his confidence and help her know how much support he will need in order to read the book successfully.

Reassess

Close observation during practice and application activities may be enough to reassure Riley's teacher that Riley has acquired the ability to decode words with the *r*-controlled vowel combination *ar*. If, in fact, he has, she may then plan a lesson in another *r*-controlled vowel combination—probably *or*. Following that, she may offer a lesson covering *er*, *ir*, and *ur* together, because those letter combinations sound exactly the same.

We also recommend using an instrument designed for frequent progress monitoring such as DIBELS-NWF and measures of oral reading fluency that are described in Chapter 6. As the student masters more and more phonic elements and word parts, he will demonstrate steady progress on the DIBELS measures.

Conclusion

Word recognition is key to unlocking texts and allowing readers to understand what authors are trying to communicate. Some children learn to read words nearly effortlessly. However, most children need explicit instruction and others need extensive support. Because vocabulary development, reading comprehension, and overall academic success rely on word recognition, we must identify students who are likely to struggle and provide them with powerful interventions. These interventions include teaching the common letter-sound correspondences, building skills in sounding out regular words, teaching irregular words, providing students with ample opportunities to apply their word skills by reading accessible texts, and strengthening their ability to decode increasingly complex words.

Meaning Vocabulary

We recently visited a sixth-grade class as the teacher, Martha Zetzel, worked with a group of seven struggling readers. After reading an article about dinosaurs, the group had a discussion. Here's an excerpt:

MS. ZETZEL: Lisa, please remind us of the question you asked before we started to read. Then read the part that answers your question.

LISA: What did dinosaurs eat? That was my question. [*She scans the article*.] Here's the answer: "Some dinosaurs ate other animals of prey and others were vegetarians, eating only plants."

MS. ZETZEL: Okay. Now, explain what you learned in your own words.

LISA: Well, I don't get it. I thought they eat other animals, but this says they pray.

TODD: That's silly. Animals can't pray!

LISA: I know, but that's what it says. Anyhow, I thought dinosaurs ate

> animals, but it says here they are vegetarians and eat only plants.
>
> **MS. ZETZEL:** Anyone else? Who can explain what Lisa just read?
>
> From this excerpt, we can tell that although Lisa could say the words correctly, she didn't understand what all of them meant. We watched for a while longer and realized that her classmates were also having problems understanding what the words meant.

Vocabulary is a major challenge for most struggling readers. There are many struggling readers who are like Lisa—they can say the word but do not know what it means. Competent readers can generally say the words and know their meanings. This is usually not the case for struggling readers.

We deal with issues related to learning to pronounce words in other chapters: phonological/phonemic awareness in Chapter 3, word recognition in Chapter 4, and fluency in Chapter 6. In Chapter 2 we discuss oral language, the foundation for all aspects of literacy. In this chapter, we focus on helping struggling readers develop and expand their meaning vocabularies—words they understand when they hear them or meet them in print, as well as words they can use correctly when they speak and write (even if they don't yet know how to spell them).

What Do We Know About Vocabulary?

Without comprehension, reading is just saying words or sounds. To be literate, one must understand the meaning of words, whether they are written or spoken. As we read we may come across words whose meaning eludes us. Often we can figure out the likely meaning from the context, using clues from the rest of the sentence or paragraph. Sometimes we decide it doesn't matter whether we know the meaning of a particular word; we just read on. But clearly, the larger our meaning vocabulary, the more we understand as we read and listen.

Our understanding of words comes from listening and from reading. We noted in Chapter 2 that some students may come to school with limited oral language or with oral language that doesn't match the language used in school and in books. So, one of our jobs is to help students increase their meaning vocabulary by exposing them to many listening and reading experiences.

We can think of vocabulary as oral vocabulary and reading vocabulary (National Reading Panel, 2000). One's reading vocabulary grows out of one's oral vocabulary. That is, we usually listen and speak before we read and write. And we usually are able to read and write only words that are already in our oral vocabularies. This is certainly true of beginning readers. As you become a better reader, you increase your vocabulary through wide reading.

There are many words in the English language (Stahl, 2004). It has been estimated (Nagy & Herman, 1987) that the average high school senior's vocabulary is made up of about 40,000 words. Considering that most kindergartners probably come to school knowing 2,000 to 3,000 words, students add a staggering number of words to their vocabularies during their school years—upwards of 3,000 a year—seven each and every day. How do students learn this astounding number of words?

How Do Students Acquire Meaning Vocabulary?

Students learn oral and print vocabulary in a variety of ways (Beck & McKeown, 1991l; Blachowicz & Fisher, 2000; McKeown & Curtis, 1987; Nagy, 1988). Therefore, no one approach will work for all students or even for any individual student (National Reading Panel, 2000). Whether you're teaching one or 100 students, a combination of approaches is necessary. That said, most children build their oral and print vocabularies sufficiently through ordinary exposure to language and print outside of school, along with instruction in school (Beck et al., 2002).

Struggling readers, however, do not acquire vocabulary so successfully. Because they lack the oral language ability most students bring to school—or because of physical, sociological, or environmental conditions—struggling readers have to work harder than other children to increase their vocabularies. And we have to work more diligently to provide the additional instruction they need.

First, let's look at the ways students acquire oral and print vocabularies. Then we will show you how to use that knowledge, along with a strong instructional plan, to help struggling readers.

- **Students learn some words through wide reading, discussion, and life experiences** (Fielding, Wilson, & Anderson, 1986; Nagy & Herman, 1987). Struggling readers often can't acquire meaning vocabulary this way for a variety of reasons. First, because they are unable to read well, they don't want to read, and therefore they do not learn words from wide reading. Second, because of their limited oral vocabulary they have few chances to increase their vocabulary through discussions with older students or adults. Finally, their life experiences may not have given them concepts and language that match what's emphasized in school.

- **Students learn some words by developing an awareness of words** (Cooper, 2006). For struggling readers to increase their vocabularies, they must increase their awareness of words through activities that require them to think about words and their meanings. For example, they may discuss interesting or unusual words they hear or encounter in reading.

- **Students learn some words through direct instruction** (Beck, McKeown, & Omanson, 1987; Graves, 1986, 1987; Stahl & Fairbanks, 1986). Direct instruction involves selecting specific words from a text and teaching those words before students read the text, by either providing the meaning or leading students to infer the meaning. The words should relate to the key ideas in the text and be useful in future reading. Sometimes instruction with groups of words that are related in meaning may take place after a text has been read.

- **Students learn some words by learning vocabulary-related skills** (Blachowicz & Fisher, 2004). Vocabulary-related skills include using knowledge of prefixes, suffixes, and inflected endings to figure out the meaning of words; understanding base words and root words; recognizing contractions and compound words. Students should be taught each of these skills in isolation and then be taught a strategy for applying the skill to unfamiliar words while reading, such as looking for familiar word parts in unfamiliar words.

In the remainder of this chapter, we focus on the process of using these ideas about how meaning vocabulary is acquired to teach struggling readers systematically.

Developing a Plan for Helping Struggling Readers Increase Their Meaning Vocabulary

There are three important steps to developing an effective plan to help struggling readers increase their meaning vocabulary. Each one reflects the best that we know from current research:

1. Build an ongoing, daily awareness of words.

2. Apply the intervention framework to meaning vocabulary.

3. Provide vocabulary follow-up activities after reading.

Build an Ongoing, Daily Awareness of Words

Since struggling readers are less aware of words and their meanings than are other readers, we must plan specific events and activities to build their consciousness. Here are some ideas to carry out on an ongoing basis to keep students thinking about word meanings.

Bulletin Boards Ask students to share interesting words they have heard or read. From there, have them define the word, use it in a sentence orally, and then write the word down and post it on a special bulletin board. The displays can be topical or thematic such as the sample shown on page 81. From time to time, discuss with the group words on the board. Encourage students to use the words while speaking and writing. Schedule a time each day for students to add new words.

Word Banks and Word Books You can also use *word banks* or *word books* to help struggling readers become more conscious of words. Word banks are files in which students keep cards containing words that interest them or new words they have learned. A word book is a notebook or student-made book that serves the same purpose. We've found that young students enjoy collecting words in word banks, but older students prefer word books because they make them feel more grown-up. Students of all ages, however, enjoy personalizing banks and books by decorating them. From time to time, have conferences with individual students about their collections or schedule a time for small groups to share and discuss their collections.

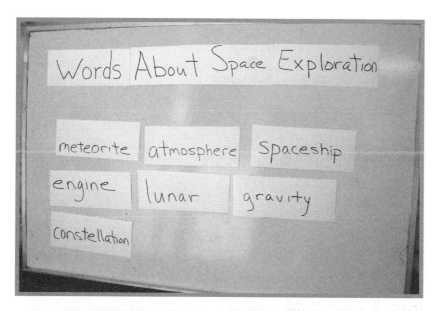

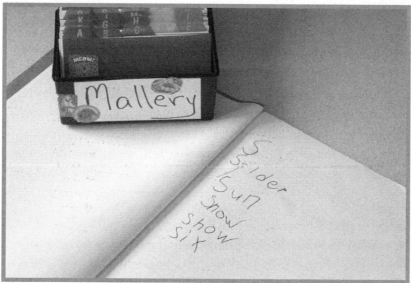

Top: A bulletin board showing vocabulary words related to space exploration.

Bottom: Mallery's word bank and a word book

Wide Reading Struggling readers are not apt to read widely on their own, so you need to help them establish the habit. We've found that the best way to entice readers is to provide a variety of reading materials, which students themselves can help you gather, such as comic books, newspaper cartoons, brochures with directions for making things, driver training manuals, short stories and articles from magazines and newspapers, CD-ROMs, and computer games. Regardless of the format, materials should relate to students' interests. You can determine student interests through casual conversation or with an inventory made up of questions such as:

- What sports do you like to play or watch on television?
- What is your favorite movie? Tell me about it.
- What kind of music do you like?
- Do you have a hobby? (Building things? Sewing? Cooking? Collecting stamps?)
- What kinds of stories do you like to read or hear?
- What are your favorite topics to read about in magazines, in books, and on the Internet?

Traditional book reports usually do not stimulate wide reading, whereas talking about books does. Plus, talking about books is something everyone can do and often stimulates others to read. So, provide time every day for students to talk to one another and with you about what they have read. You should share what you are reading, also, which sends a strong message that reading is not just something they are required to do, but something many adults do by choice.

Read Aloud No matter how old your students are, you should read aloud to them regularly. When students hear text read aloud, they are exposed to a wide variety of words and can often derive meaning of unfamiliar words from context. Choose reading material based on students' suggestions or interests. Practice your oral reading to ensure that you can hold listeners' attention. As you read to students, be aware of their facial expressions, which will tip you off if a word or concept is not understood and allow you to explore or explain that word or concept before going on. Throughout the day, use words from what you have read aloud. With frequent exposure, new words will become familiar. You will

The Struggling Reader: Interventions That Work

likely hear students try them out while speaking. And you will feel rewarded when you see students recognizing those words in print.

Daily Discussion of Words Allot time each day for students to talk about words from the bulletin board, word banks or word books, or Read Aloud. You may have a one-on-one discussion with a student or bring together a small group of struggling readers for a discussion. If you do the latter, lead the discussions until students are comfortable and confident carrying them out on their own, on a daily basis.

Apply the Intervention Framework to Meaning Vocabulary

Recall the intervention instructional framework that we introduced in Chapter 1, which is made up of five steps: (1) assess and diagnose, (2) teach/reteach, (3) practice, (4) apply, and (5) reassess. This framework can be used to teach key concept vocabulary before students read text, as well as the vocabulary-related skills and strategies mentioned earlier. In this section, we describe how to do both.

Teaching Key Concept Vocabulary Before Reading If properly done, teaching *key concept vocabulary* before reading can enhance overall comprehension as well as increase vocabulary (Baumann & Kame'enui, 2004; Stahl & Fairbanks, 1986). Here are five guidelines to follow:

- **Select six to eight words related to the key concepts in the text.** Read the text in advance of your instruction. Research has shown that students do not need to know every word in a text to understand the text (Nagy, 1988). Therefore, choose six to eight key words to teach that are not defined by the author but are so critical to understanding that comprehension would be impossible without knowing them. Key words should come from the story line in narrative text or the main ideas in expository text. For example, if your students are reading *Gladiator* (Watkins, 1997), select words such as *arena, consul, legionaries,* and *ocrea* because they are closely related to the life and times of gladiators. A group of related words is easier to learn than a group of unrelated words and is especially helpful to struggling readers.

- **Make sure the words are going to be useful in reading other texts** (Beck et al., 2002). Sometimes words that relate to key concepts in a particular text may be unlikely to turn up in other texts. For example, if you consider the words from *Gladiator*, *arena*, *consul*, and *legionaries* might be met in other texts. However, *ocrea*, which is a metal leg guard, probably won't. In fact, it may not be necessary to preteach that word for students to understand the book's important ideas.

- **Know the context in which the words appear.** Because the meanings of some words vary depending on their context, it's a good idea to teach only the meaning students need to understand the text you are about to give them. Later, once students have had multiple exposures to the word, they should be able to understand its meaning in a variety of contexts. For example, in order to comprehend *Gladiator* fully, students need to know that the word *arena* means the sand-covered fighting area in the amphitheater. Further exposures to the word in other contexts should allow students to expand their definition to include "a modern sports area" and "a sphere of interest."

- **Provide interactive instruction that builds connections for students.** Copying dictionary definitions and writing sentences that confirm understanding of those definitions have no place in the vocabulary instruction of any student—certainly not those who struggle. Words are best learned when they are taught interactively, meaning new words should be connected to words and concepts the student already knows, in the context of a sentence, paragraph, or longer text.

- **Use graphic representations during instruction.** Struggling readers learn more readily when information is presented graphically, using a representation such as a word map (shown in Figure 5.1) or a Venn diagram (shown in Figure 5.2). We discuss representations in depth later.

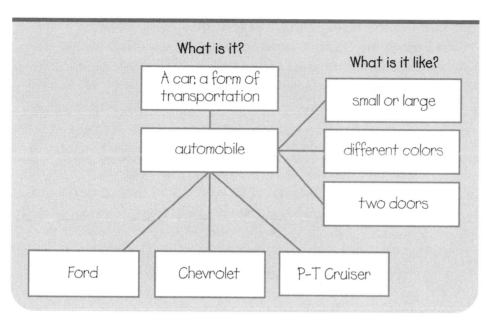

FIGURE 5.1 Sample word map

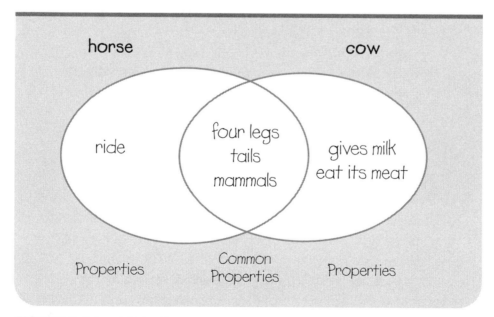

FIGURE 5.2 Sample Venn diagram

Sample Lesson Using the Intervention Framework
With Struggling Sixth-Grade Students
Now let's look at a lesson, based on the book *Gladiator*, that Ms. Zetzel might teach to the seven struggling readers in her class, using the intervention framework.

- **Assess and Diagnose** Before meeting with the group, read *Gladiator's* first chapter, "Ancient Rome." Identify key words that support the chapter's major concepts: *exploited, empire, military, civilization, dethroned,* and *violence.*

   Gather the group together, providing each with a copy of the book, and direct students to find each word in the chapter, read the sentence in which it appears, and tell what they know about it. This gives you an idea of which words students know well, know somewhat, and don't know at all, so that you can determine how much support they'll need during instruction.

   Every student is likely to have inadequate or inaccurate understanding of at least some of the target words. In a small group, you will be able to remember which students stumbled on which words and focus attention on them during the lesson.

- **Teach** Display the following paragraph on an overhead transparency or piece of chart paper.

   > The people of Rome knew about the *violence* that caused death for many of its citizens. The *military*, made up of young soldiers, *exploited* or abused nearly everyone who was poor. Through wars, even some very powerful rulers were *dethroned*. Even though this was a *civilization* that knew much about art and science, it was an *empire* of death and pain for many.

   Read the paragraph aloud to the group. Then give each student a 3-by-5 card with a key concept word on one side and its definition on the other. As you distribute the cards, pronounce each word and read aloud the definition. Read the paragraph aloud again, stopping at key concept words to allow individual students to say the word and tell or read its definition from the card.

   Have students exchange cards and call on one student to read aloud the paragraph's first sentence. Have the student holding the card with the key concept word say the word and give the definition. Continue through the paragraph, with students taking turns reading the sentences, the key concept words, and their definitions, and exchanging cards each time they finish the paragraph. Continue this procedure only until you are confident that students know the meaning of the new words.

- **Practice** Duplicate each card to create a two-card set of each key concept word. Shuffle the cards and have students take turns drawing a card, reading the word, and giving the meaning. Don't spend more time on practice than necessary; students should move quickly and remain focused. The point is for them to understand the word sufficiently when they meet it in the chapter they are going to read.

- **Apply** Now students are ready to read the whole chapter because they know the key concept vocabulary necessary to understand it.

    If you think students would benefit from further help, do activities for accessing or building background for reading, which are discussed in detail in Chapter 7. For *Gladiator*, you might have students make K-W-L charts about what they expect to learn in the book. (See Figure 5.3.) Students should then read the chapter silently and summarize it orally. If they are unable to summarize, do it for them, incorporating as many key concept words as you can. Then ask students to try again, using your summary as a model. If students are still unable to summarize using the new vocabulary words, ask them to locate a sentence containing a key concept word, read it aloud, and tell the meaning.

What I Know	What I Want to Learn	What I Learned

FIGURE 5.3 Sample K-W-L chart

As you observe students practicing and applying strategies, be on the lookout for needs. In this case, for example, you may learn that your struggling readers need lessons later on summarizing after you've completed the one on new vocabulary. Remember—lessons for struggling readers need to be focused and quick paced.

- **Reassess** Have students write a paragraph about the chapter, using each of the new words. Read or have students read aloud each paragraph in order to judge whether words were used correctly. If they were not, reteach them based on the extent to which students need them. If the words recur in the books students are reading, then you should reteach them. If not, there is little point in belaboring them.

COMMENTS: This lesson is one example of the direct, explicit teaching necessary for struggling readers to increase their vocabularies. Remember, because struggling readers have more limited vocabularies than competent readers, independent strategies such as using context to arrive at word meanings can be much more difficult for them. Preteaching key concept words and strategies for figuring out their meaning makes reading a more successful experience.

Figure 5.4 presents a variety of routines that can be used for teaching vocabulary directly and explicitly, before and during reading. Some can also be used after reading to expand vocabulary by helping students make connections between words that are conceptually or linguistically related. The key to success is using these routines systematically and repeatedly.

Routine	Procedures	Comments
ORAL CONTEXT	1. Choose key concept words and create sentences in which the word is used in a context similar to the text students are going to read. 2. Give each student one or two cards, each containing one of the words to be taught. Read each word card aloud with students. 3. Read the sentences or scenario aloud, asking each student to hold up his or her card when he or she hears the word on it. 4. Discuss the word's meaning.	This procedure is similar to the one used in the sample intervention lesson described on pages 86-87. It is direct, keeps students actively involved, and moves from oral language to print.
TEXT READ ALOUDS	1. Put words from a new text on individual cards. Pronounce all words with students; have students pronounce the words after you. 2. Read aloud the text; have students hold up the appropriate word card when they hear their word. 3. Discuss each word's meanings as students hold up cards.	This routine is similar to the Oral Context routine except it is based on words students are going to read in pre-selected texts.
POSSIBLE SENTENCES	1. From the text to be read, select six to eight unknown words along with four to eight words students know. 2. Put words on individual cards. 3. Have students work alone or in pairs to create sentences, using at least one new word in each sentence. If writing is difficult for students, they may dictate the sentences with you serving as scribe. Have students read the text. 4. Return to the sentences students wrote to verify whether words were used correctly.	This procedure, developed by Stahl and Kapinus (1991), helps students build rich contexts for words and develop word relationships.
GRAPHIC REPRESENTATIONS such as word maps (Figure 5.1, Figure 5.2, Figure 5.5, and Figure 5.6)	1. Identify unfamiliar words from a text students will read. You can determine whether the words are unfamiliar by using a procedure such as the one used for *Gladiator* on page 86. 2. Select an appropriate graphic representation based on how the meanings of the words are related. 3. Have students work with you to create the graphic.	Graphic representations help struggling readers remember the words by illustrating connections between them.
TEXT TALK	1. Preview the text and identify key concept words to teach before students read. 2. Have a discussion in which you help students connect the word as used in the text to be read to other contexts or situations. (See sample Text Talk in Figure 5.7.)	This routine was developed by Beck and McKeown (2001) for use with young readers, but it also works well with older, struggling readers.

FIGURE 5.4 Routines for direct teaching of vocabulary to struggling readers

Key Word	Other Words That Mean the Same
empty	blank, vacant
shy	bashful, coy, diffident, modest
make	construct, fabricate, fashion, manufacture, shape

FIGURE 5.5 Sample word chart

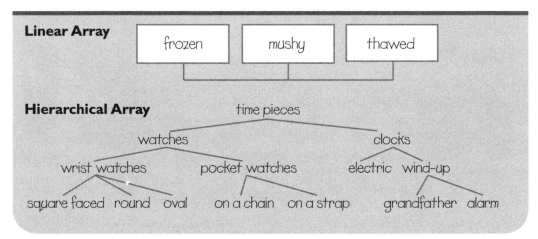

FIGURE 5.6 Sample linear array and hierarchical array

Text Talk Script

In the book *Officer Buckle and Gloria*, Officer Buckle had a rule about never standing on a swivel chair. Swivel means it turns around. Let's say the word together.

Other things can swivel besides chairs. Can you tell me something else that can swivel? (*Some rides at the fair swivel from side to side.*) Show how you can swivel around while standing in place.

Let's say the word together.

In the story, Officer Buckle gave commands to Gloria. *Commands* are orders or directions. Say the word with me.

Who sometimes gives you commands (parents, teacher, principal)?

Who do you give commands to (pet, brother, sister)?

What do they do when you give the commands?

FIGURE 5.7 Sample Text Talk script to be used after reading the picture book *Officer Buckle and Gloria* (Rathmann, 1995) to build understanding of the words *swivel* and *commands*.

Teaching Vocabulary-Related Strategies and Skills We have just shown you how to teach key concept vocabulary before having students read a particular piece of text. Now we present teaching strategies and skills that will help students become independent learners of new words.

Many struggling readers have no trouble applying a skill in isolation, but they cannot apply the skill while reading extended text. For example, a student might be able to tell you that *un* in the word *unhappy* means "not"—but be unable to use that knowledge when trying to figure out the word *uncommon*. What these students need is a five-step strategy for dealing with words they don't know, such as the one in Figure 5.8, which we summarize here:

> Try sounding out the word. If that results in a word you know that fits the context, great. Keep reading. If phonics doesn't work, look for a word part, such as a prefix, and think about what it means. If that doesn't work, read to the end of the sentence, thinking about what it means and what word might fit. Reread the sentence. If these methods don't work and you need the meaning of the word to make sense of the text, ask someone or use a dictionary.

The strategy in Figure 5.8 for identifying word meaning should be taught using the intervention framework (assess and diagnose, teach/reteach, practice, apply, and reassess) with students in grades three and above who are most likely ready to begin applying each step. Chances are, however, that younger struggling readers won't be ready. For example, using word parts to figure out meaning is probably too advanced for them. Therefore, adapt lessons to match where students are developmentally.

It's important to remember that here, unlike in the last section, the goal is not to teach specific words. Instead, we show you how to teach a strategy described in Figure 5.8 to help students become independent readers. In the sample lesson that follows, students first learn the prefix *un* and then apply that knowledge to infer word meanings independently.

- **Assess and Diagnose** Show students a familiar word, ask them for its meaning, add a prefix to the word, and then ask them for the meaning of the newly created word. For example, display the word *tie*, have students read it aloud, and ask them to tell you what it means. Then display the word *untie*. Have students read it aloud, tell the meaning, and explain how the prefix *un-* affected the meaning. Repeat with another prefix, such as *re-*. If students

FIGURE 5.8 A five-step strategy for identifying word meanings

are uncertain about how the prefix changes meaning, teach a lesson in the skill. Even if they understand the meaning of a particular prefix, they may not be able to apply that knowledge to figuring out a new word.

- **Teach/Reteach** Model the use of the strategy shown in Figure 5.8. For example, if you have recently taught the prefix *re-*, display a sentence containing a word you think students will not recognize, such as "The sentence was hard to follow, so the teacher said I should restate it." Model the steps: apply phonics and show how that doesn't work for you. Then look for word parts and note the prefix *re-* and the base word *state*. Explain that the prefix tells you something is done again but you don't know what that has to do with "a state." Read the sentence aloud, thinking about the words *again* and *state*. Then model remembering that *state* can also mean "to say." Read the sentence with that meaning—"say again"—and read on because the sentence now makes sense to you.

Continue the lessons using other words with the prefix *re-* or other prefixes, including examples that students find in books or magazines. Create a poster based on Figure 5.8, display it prominently, and refer to it frequently. Whenever a student comes to you to ask the meaning of a word, ask, "Have you used the strategy from the poster? What step are you on? Tell me about it." Eventually, students won't come to you until they are at step 5. Giving students individual copies of Figure 5.8 to refer to as they read is also a good idea.

When teaching the strategy, be careful about emphasizing correct pronunciation over correct meaning. Remember, your purpose is to help students become independent in figuring out the meanings of unfamiliar words. When they read silently, it doesn't always matter if they can pronounce the word correctly—what matters most is whether they understand it.

Whether you're teaching prefixes, suffixes, base words, or root words, use the method described above. Specifically, start with what students know about the word part and then apply strategies for figuring out words that contain that part.

If you've carried out lessons described in Chapter 4, students should be comfortable trying Steps 1 and 2 in Figure 5.8. But to use Step 3, they need to be taught useful word parts. A word of caution, though: To avoid overwhelming struggling readers, teach only those **prefixes** and **suffixes** that occur often in texts they choose or are expected to read. Figure 5.9 presents the prefixes and suffixes that researchers have determined merit attention in instruction.

Prefixes	Suffixes
Meaning "not" un- unhappy dis- disrespectful in-, im- inactive impossible non- nonresistant ir- irresponsible	**Plural** -s, -es girls, boxes **Tense** -s jumps -ed jumped -ing jumping
Meaning "back" or "again" re- revisit	**Meaning "like"** -ly sisterly
Meaning "do the opposite of" un- untie dis- disassemble	**Meaning "one who performs a specialized action"** -er, -or swimmer, actor
Meaning "in" or "into" in-, im- indoors	**Used to form comparative degree with adjectives** -er darker
Meaning "into" or "within" en-, em- entangle	**Meaning "act of doing"** -tion absorption -ion construction -ation operation -ition demolition
Meaning "too much" over- overdose	**Meaning "susceptible," "capable," or "worth"** -able debatable -ible collectible
Meaning "wrong" mis- misspell	**Meaning "of" or "relating to"** -al, -ial parental, facial
	Meaning "consisting of" or "inclined toward" -y furry, sleepy
	Meaning "state," "quality," "condition," or "degree" -ness brightness

FIGURE 5.9 Prefixes and suffixes that merit attention in instruction. Accounts for nearly 50 percent of all prefixed words (Graves, 1987). Based on White, Sowell, and Yanagihara (1989)

Provide Vocabulary Follow-Up Activities After Reading

So far we've shown you how to help struggling readers develop stronger meaning vocabularies by building awareness of words *before* reading and applying a strategy for figuring out unfamiliar words *during* reading. Next we provide vocabulary follow-up activities for use *after* reading. Most of these activities expand and extend vocabulary for struggling readers by helping them build connections between and among words from the text they read.

The five routines for before reading presented in Figure 5.4 (oral context, text Read Alouds, possible sentences, graphic presentations, and text talk) can also be used after reading. Here are four more activities that are particularly appropriate for use following reading. Each one is designed to enrich understanding of a word by encouraging students to think about other words that have the same meaning, or have an opposite meaning, or share a feature with or belong to the same category of words, or connect words that are related to the same broad concept.

Synonyms Blachowicz and Fisher (2004) recommend using activities focusing on synonyms to help struggling readers expand their vocabularies. Here is an example: After reading a text, give pairs of students a list of words related to the content of that text. Have partners work together to find *synonyms* for each word on the list, using a dictionary and/or their background knowledge. If students don't know how to use the dictionary to carry out the task or don't have the

necessary background knowledge, give them a dictionary and show them how to use it. From there, consider having students create a synonym web such as the one shown in Figure 5.10. This activity can also be carried out by having students find antonyms for the words on their list.

Students can then discuss the words in small groups, add the words to their word banks or word books (described on pages 80–81), and/or create individual synonym/antonym dictionaries.

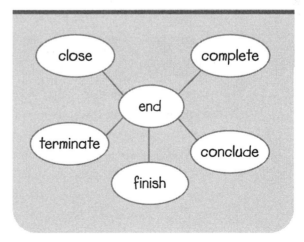

FIGURE 5.10 Sample synonym web

Semantic Feature Analysis Semantic feature analysis was developed to help students look at how related words differ and how they are alike (Johnson & Pearson, 1984). Use the following procedure to help readers construct a semantic feature analysis grid like the one shown in Figure 5.11.

1. Select a category or class of words such as "tools." Begin by listing one tool, such as hammer, on the left side of the grid.

2. Have students give features of that tool, such as used for nailing things, wooden handle, claw to extract nails, heavy. List the features across the top of the grid.

3. Continue building the grid by adding tools and features. With each tool, if the feature students mention is already showing on the grid, just put a plus sign in the square under that feature.

Birds	Have feathers	Eaten by people	Fly	Swim
duck	+	+	+	+
chicken	+	+	+	–
turkey	+	+	+	–
parrot	+	?	+	–
ostrich	+	+	–	?

+ = yes
– = no
? = not sure

FIGURE 5.11 Sample semantic feature analysis grid

4. Have students think about each tool and each feature. Put a plus (+) in a square to indicate that tool has a feature. Put a minus (-) if the tool does not have the feature. You may also indicate both plus and minus if students tell you some tools have a particular feature and some do not. If students do not know whether a particular tool has a feature, put a question mark in the square. Students can search for this information later.

5. Return to the grid to further discuss how some tools are similar to or different from one another. For example, there may be two tools that look different but serve the same basic purpose, such as a slot screwdriver and a Phillips head screwdriver.

In addition to expanding vocabulary, the semantic feature analysis can be used to structure a review of a chapter from a content-area book. For a detailed discussion, see *Literacy: Helping Children Construct Meaning*, Sixth Edition, by J. David Cooper (2006).

List-Group-Label This technique was devised by Taba more than 30 years ago (Taba, 1967), and is presented here with some variations. Teach students the technique by leading them through it a few times, as described below. Eventually, they should be able to do it independently, with a partner, or in a self-directed small group.

1. After students have read a text, have them identify the words that are most important to understanding the content. For example, if they have just read an article about natural disasters, they might suggest words such as *volcano, hurricane, flood,* and *drought.*

2. Have students continue to suggest words related to any of these words, from the text or their background knowledge, and record them in no particular order. If a word is suggested that does not relate, don't accept it and explain why.

3. When you have a collection of words related to the concept of natural disasters, guide students to put related words into groups and label the groups. Not only does this activity help students see how concepts, and the words for those concepts, are related, but it also provides a good review of the text's main ideas and, therefore, reinforces comprehension.

4. Alter the activity by first having students suggest categories of ideas related to disasters. For example, they might suggest location, season, duration, risk to human life, and so forth. Then have students give words that belong in each of these categories such as *forests*, *oceans*, and *Florida* for location; or *winter* for season.

5. When students are comfortable carrying out the technique under your guidance, have them work independently.

Word Sorts Word Sorts are another effective activity to help students expand their understanding of the meaning of words by considering how groups of words are related (McKenna, 2004). After students have learned a number of words, put the words on individual cards and mix them up. Then, working on their own or in partners, have students sort the words into categories. Figure 5.12 presents an example of a Word Sort done by some struggling fourth-grade readers.

Colors	People	Animals	Feelings
red	Germans	elephants	happy
green	Americans	monkeys	sad
yellow	Greeks	dogs	scared
magenta	nomads	cats	frightened
	astronauts	gerbils	

FIGURE 5.12 Word Sort by struggling fourth-grade readers

Conclusion

Struggling readers typically do not expand their meaning vocabularies on their own. They need help. Teachers must take positive, consistent, systematic steps. We must help students become conscious of words they see and hear, in and outside of school. We must provide direct instruction using the intervention framework to teach key concept vocabulary before reading, to teach a strategy for independently identifying word meanings, and to teach skills that can be applied when using the strategy. Finally we must give students follow-up activities after reading to expand and deepen their understanding of individual words and word groups related to key concepts. We cannot rely on instruction that works for most learners. We must build vocabulary every single day using intense, focused, consistent instruction. If we do, the payoff is terrific: readers whose struggles lessen as they become independent readers.

Professional Resources for Building Vocabulary

The following books contain additional ideas for teaching vocabulary to struggling readers.

- *Words, Words, Words: Teaching Vocabulary in Grades 4–12* by J. Allen, Stenhouse

- *Vocabulary Instruction: Research to Practice* edited by J. F. Baumann and E. J. Kame'enui, Guilford

- *Bringing Words to Life: Robust Vocabulary Instruction* by I. L. Beck, M. G. McKeown, and L. Kucan, Guilford

- *Teaching Vocabulary in All Classrooms* by C. Blachowicz and P. Fisher, Prentice Hall

- *The Vocabulary-Enriched Classroom: Practices for Improving the Reading Performance of All Students in Grades 3 and Up* edited by C. C. Block and J. N. Mangieri, Scholastic

- *What Reading Research Tells Us About Children With Diverse Learning Needs* edited by D. C. Simmons and E. J. Kame'enui, Erlbaum

- *Vocabulary Development* by S. A. Stahl, Brookline Books

CHAPTER 6

Reading Fluency

CASE STUDY

Rosa Gomez is a fourth-grade teacher at Central Elementary School. Recently, she assessed each student in her class for fluency and most are reading at about 115 correct words per minute, which is normal for this grade. However, six students lack fluency, though their problems are not the same. Elisha, Jamal, and Caitlin decode accurately but read slowly. They are still reading only about 50 words correctly per minute when reading in fourth-grade text.

Natalie reads accurately and quickly, but she doesn't seem to know when to pause. She doesn't pay attention to punctuation and uses a very flat voice. Her oral reading lacks expression. Furthermore, when Ms. Gomez asks her questions about what she has read, Natalie is usually not able to answer them.

Will and Sandra frequently substitute one word for another when reading orally, such as *was* for *saw*. They also have problems decoding words with traditionally tricky spelling patterns, such as *freight*.

Ms. Gomez realizes that she needs to pay particular attention to the fluency needs of these six students. In her professional reading, she has learned that fluency can be boosted with strategically planned activities that focus on students' reading rate, accuracy, and expression. She has also learned that fluency problems make comprehension difficult—it's hard to pay attention to meaning when reading is slow and labored. So she makes plans to increase the fluency of these students.

What Is Fluency?

The more one does something, the better one becomes at it. Repeated practice of a task under different conditions helps a novice become more expert. In other words, he or she becomes more fluent.

Here's an example. Consider a young child learning to ride a bike. While some kids become skillful bike riders by themselves, most benefit from some help. At first, the task is difficult and requires tremendous concentration. The child falls a lot and may become discouraged. An older child or an adult may teach specific skills such as pushing off, pedaling, or leaning into turns. Lots of encouragement also helps, although the joy of being able to ride independently is often incentive enough. Eventually, the child succeeds in wobbling down the road for the first time, most likely with a few falls. However, with practice, the falls become less frequent, the wobbling decreases, and the speed increases. The child tries more complicated turns and stops. This process of going from a faltering beginning to skillful mastery can be thought of as a growth in bike-riding fluency.

Like struggling bike-riding, some children's oral reading is so wobbly and slow that, by the time they reach the end of a sentence, they have forgotten the beginning. They are so burdened by the decoding task that they cannot think about the meaning of the words they are reading. They sigh with relief when they have said all the words. But we all know that "saying words" is not reading. Natalie, whose word recognition was accurate and rapid, still didn't seem to understand what she had said—perhaps because she didn't pay attention to cues from punctuation.

What Is Reading Fluency?

Reading *fluency* is defined as rapid, efficient, accurate application of word-recognition skills that permit a reader to construct the meaning, or comprehend. Fluent reading also includes expressive oral reading and evidence that rapid, efficient, accurate application of word-recognition skills is used during silent reading. (Chard, Vaughn, & Tyler, 2002; Dowhower, 1991).

Why Is Reading Fluency Important?

Fluent reading has been recognized as an important element of reading proficiency since early in the last century (Huey, 1908). It represents, as Harris and Hodges (1995) noted, the "freedom from word identification problems that might hinder comprehension" (p. 85). In other words, when students read fluently, they don't focus exclusively on an author's individual words; instead, they focus on the author's overall message. In this sense, fluency serves as a bridge between accurate decoding and understanding the text (Pikulski & Chard, 2005; Rasinski & Hoffman, 2003). A significant positive relationship between reading fluency and reading comprehension has been clearly established (Pinnell et al., 1995).

In order for reading to be efficient and effective, the reader cannot focus attention simultaneously on decoding and comprehending. Think of trying to pat your head and rub your stomach at the same time—you know how tough that is! Though the non-fluent reader can alternate attention between the two processes, constructing meaning *always* requires undisrupted attention. So if a learner's attention is focused mostly on decoding words, nothing much is left for constructing and responding to the meaning of a text. Conversely, if the non-fluent reader's attention is on comprehension, word recognition falters. Therefore, fluency is essential for high levels of reading achievement.

A second reason that fluency is important is that fluent readers are more likely to read than non-fluent readers. Think about something you don't do well—perhaps cooking. You probably don't ever choose to cook because it's too hard and no fun. Non-fluent readers find reading difficult, even punishing, so they don't choose to read and, therefore, do not enjoy the benefits of reading, such as increased vocabulary, more sophisticated understanding of the world, and fluency. This can lead to a trajectory of poor achievement that grows increasingly difficult to reverse as students move up the grades (Stanovich, 1986). It is a self-perpetuating problem—the student doesn't read because he doesn't do it well; the student doesn't improve in reading because he doesn't read.

How Do Readers Become Fluent?

Understanding how readers become fluent will help you plan instruction for your struggling readers. LaBerge and Samuels (1974) theorize that readers gain fluency as they increase their ***automaticity*** with the ***subskills*** of early reading such as letter-sound knowledge. In other words, as students learn to recognize letters, corresponding sounds, word parts, and words automatically, their fluency with connected texts grows.

Another way to look at the development of fluency is as a stage in reading development. In Chapter 4 we described the stages in Ehri's (1998) model. Fluency begins as children become increasingly familiar with the sounds that letters are likely to represent—in other words, when they reach Ehri's fully alphabetic stage. When a child is at this stage and meets an unfamiliar word (e.g., *sun*), he can assign sounds to each letter, blend the sounds together, and pronounce the word. After encountering and decoding the word several times, he can accurately and instantly identify it. He no longer needs to decode it because it has become a ***sight word***, a word recognized immediately upon seeing it. Instant, accurate, automatic reading of words leads to fluency. And, as mentioned earlier, fluency allows readers to focus their attention on comprehension rather than decoding.

As readers move into Ehri's consolidated alphabetic stage, they develop another decoding skill that leads to fluency—the instant recognition of spelling patterns that occur across different words. In her research, Ehri demonstrates that, in addition to recognizing sight words, repeated encounters with words allow readers to store letter patterns in their heads. For example, after students learn the spelling pattern *-ight* in one word, they "consolidate" that word in their memory, along with its corresponding sounds, for use later in reading words such as *night, sight, fright, bright,* and *plight.* This is sometimes referred to as reading by analogy. Although reading words by analogy is not as efficient as reading words by sight, it allows readers to figure out more complicated words—and with sufficient exposure these words will become sight words.

You probably recognize most words at sight, without needing to decode them. Because you are familiar with many spelling patterns, reading by analogy happens so quickly you aren't aware of it. Whether reading silently or aloud, you can focus on the text's message. When a word does stump you, you have ways to deal with it—you use context or a dictionary, or you ask a friend for help, or you skip the word entirely. Even though skipping the word is sometimes appropriate, we need to be careful about directing students to do this too freely; it could lead to a bad habit. Many children gain fluency through regular classroom instruction and their own desire to read. Struggling readers need intervention.

Applying the Intervention Framework to Reading Fluency

At the beginning stages of reading, students are figuring out the sound-symbol system. How do the marks on the page relate to sounds? How does the print stand for words? Until students have a good grasp of how the system works, attempts to build fluency are counterproductive. If you stress reading quickly, your students may focus on speed and sacrifice accuracy. They will guess at words. So, it's important to assess their fluency and then determine the best teaching approach and way to monitor progress.

With that in mind, in this section we first discuss how to apply the intervention framework to fluency. Then we give examples of lessons to address each of the fluency problems we saw in Ms. Gomez's struggling readers.

Assess and Diagnose

Assessing fluency and diagnosing fluency problems can be formal or informal. Many teachers use informal approaches starting midway through first grade, when students have sufficient knowledge of phonics, a decoding strategy such as discussed in Chapter 4, and enough high-frequency words to read connected text successfully. These informal assessments include running records or observations during independent or partner reading. If you suspect a student of having problems with fluency based on informal assessments like those, use a more formal approach.

Formal assessment of fluency should address all three fluency components: rate (the number of words read per minute), accuracy (the number of words read correctly), and *prosody* (the use of appropriate expression). Here is one procedure for assessing rate and accuracy, which is sometimes referred to as *oral reading fluency*.

1. Select three grade-level passages of 150–250 words, containing simple syntax and few proper nouns or technical words.

2. Make two photocopies of each passage, one for you to mark on and one for the student to read. If the passages contain pictures, block them out or retype the passages entirely. Students should read without the aid of art.

3. Sit in a quiet place and have the student read each passage for one minute while you mark any errors the student makes. Errors include hesitating for three seconds or more, reversing letters or words, and mispronouncing, substituting, or omitting words. Do not count hesitations of less than three seconds, additions of words, self-corrections, or rereading as errors.

4. At the end of one minute, calculate the student's fluency on each passage as correct words per minute (CWPM) by counting the number of words read and subtracting the number of errors.

5. The student's fluency is represented by the average of the three fluency scores. Determine whether the student's fluency is on target by comparing his or her score on this assessment to benchmark scores. Benchmark scores on similar procedures have been reported in the literature (e.g., Hasbrouck & Tindal, 1992; Good & Kaminski, 2002) and in state reading frameworks. Figure 6.1 shows the range of end-of-year benchmarks.

If a student's reading fluency is significantly discrepant from these guidelines (e.g., a second grader reading 43 CWPM in spring), she probably has a difficult time comprehending the text because she is paying too much attention to decoding its words. When a reader is struggling with comprehension, a fluency assessment may give you a sense of where her problem lies and a starting point for remedying it.

Rate and accuracy are only part of the fluency picture. You must also assess your students' attention to prosodic elements such as pitch, stress, loudness, and pauses indicated

Grade Level	End-of-Year Reading Fluency Rates (CWPM)
1st	70 – 90
2nd	80 – 100
3rd	100 – 120
4th	110 – 130
5th	120 – 140

FIGURE 6.1 End-of-year grade-level guidelines for reading rate and accuracy

by punctuation. Assessing prosody is difficult. Although clear procedures have not been established, we recommend creating your own rubric for assessing fluency that includes prosody, or using the Multidimensional Fluency Scale in Timothy V. Rasinski and Nancy Padak's 3-*Minute Reading Assessments: Word Recognition, Fluency & Comprehension* (2005) or the rubric established for the National Assessment of Educational Progress (NAEP). The NAEP rubric has four levels and distinguishes word-by-word reading from the reader's attention to phrases, syntax, and expression. See Figure 6.2.

Most students in mid- to late first grade will likely be at Level 2 when reading grade-level material or material at their instructional level, reading the words accurately as they develop their sight-word reading and decoding abilities. However, by the middle of second grade, students should be at or entering Level

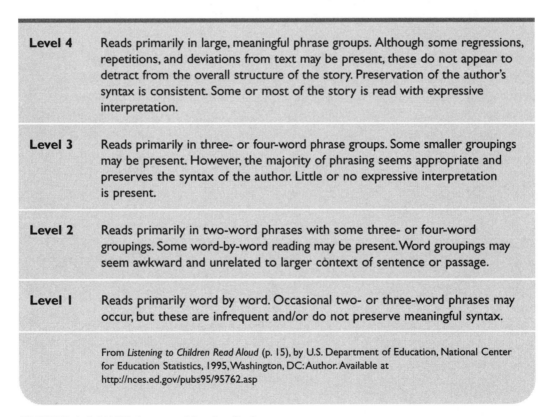

Level 4	Reads primarily in large, meaningful phrase groups. Although some regressions, repetitions, and deviations from text may be present, these do not appear to detract from the overall structure of the story. Preservation of the author's syntax is consistent. Some or most of the story is read with expressive interpretation.
Level 3	Reads primarily in three- or four-word phrase groups. Some smaller groupings may be present. However, the majority of phrasing seems appropriate and preserves the syntax of the author. Little or no expressive interpretation is present.
Level 2	Reads primarily in two-word phrases with some three- or four-word groupings. Some word-by-word reading may be present. Word groupings may seem awkward and unrelated to larger context of sentence or passage.
Level 1	Reads primarily word by word. Occasional two- or three-word phrases may occur, but these are infrequent and/or do not preserve meaningful syntax.

From *Listening to Children Read Aloud* (p. 15), by U.S. Department of Education, National Center for Education Statistics, 1995, Washington, DC: Author. Available at http://nces.ed.gov/pubs95/95762.asp

FIGURE 6.2 NAEP's Integrated Reading Performance Record Oral Reading Fluency Scale

Fluency Characteristic	Intervention Objective	Intervention Content
Slow reading in connected text	Increase reading rate	Repeated reading of familiar leveled text (See Practice step on page 109.)
Inaccurate reading of some words	Increase accuracy of reading connected texts	Repeated reading with coaching using the decoding strategy (See Chapter 4.) (See Practice step on page 109.)
Poor use of expression or attention to prosody	Improve attention to features of text that prompt expression (e.g., dialogue marks, punctuation)	Modeled reading with particular text features pointed out during shared reading (See Teach/Reteach step on page 108.)
Repeated misreadings of particular words or word types	Increase accuracy of specific words or word types	Word blending and word list reading (See Teach/Reteach step on page 108.)

FIGURE 6.3 Matching fluency characteristics with intervention targets

3, reading passages with understanding and expression. Many second graders will achieve Level 4 as the year progresses and they grow more fluent in their reading.

If a student is not making progress, he may not understand how to use the features of text, such as punctuation, to read it naturally. It may also signify that the student is still so focused on word-by-word decoding that he is unable to think about prosody. In either case, the student would benefit from intervention. For more about fluency assessment, see *The Fluent Reader: Oral Reading Strategies for Building Word Recognition, Fluency, and Comprehension* (Rasinski, 2003).

Once struggling readers move beyond the middle of first grade, formally monitor them using the procedures described earlier to measure rate and accuracy, as well as a rubric to gauge growth in prosody. As you diagnose difficulties, use the guidelines in Figure 6.3 to match students' fluency characteristics with intervention objectives and content.

Teach/Reteach

When it comes to teaching, two specific characteristics of students' fluency may warrant your attention: difficulties with attending to the prosodic elements of text and repeated difficulties with decoding specific words or word types. In this section, we address both issues.

If the problem is attending to prosodic elements of text, try modeled reading. When you model oral reading, you demonstrate how to pace reading and use expression by doing the things that all good readers do, such as attending to dialogue marks and punctuation. Having students listen to stories on tape or through a computer also works, but not as well as teacher modeling for younger and less able readers (Daly & Martens, 1994; Rose & Beattie, 1986).

Modeled oral reading can also improve students' comprehension. Students can focus on the content of the passage as they listen, before they read it independently (Monda, 1989; Rose & Beattie, 1986). We recommend having students silently read along in the text while you read aloud or while they listen to a taped reading.

If the problem is decoding specific words or word types, try word blending and word-list reading. For decoding problems, use direct teaching of words on a list. Studies in which teachers had students practice reading lists of words that they were to later encounter in connected texts consistently resulted in increased fluency (Fleisher, Jenkins, & Pany, 1979–80; Levy, Abello, & Lysynchuk, 1997), although there was no increase in comprehension. However, preteaching the meanings of words for a particular text can have a positive effect on comprehension (Tan & Nicholson, 1997). See Chapter 5 for general information on teaching meaning vocabulary and Chapter 7 for guidelines on selecting and preteaching new vocabulary to improve comprehension. Here are two procedures to help students overcome difficulties with specific words or word types and, in the process, become more fluent.

- **Word blending** Select five to seven words that students do not know. For example—*past, fast, last, list, mist, must.* Displaying one word at a time, move your finger under each letter and say its sound. Blend the letter sounds quickly to say the whole word. Repeat the process with students. Encourage students to verbalize the difference between sounding out the word and saying it fast, and talk about how saying it fast helps them read fluently. (See Chapter 4 for more on word blending.)

- **Word-list reading** Lists should be compiled of words with similar spelling patterns that the student struggles to read. For example, if the student is struggling with the spelling pattern *igh* as in *sight*, include words such as *sight*, *tight*, *fright*, *bright*, and *night* on the list. Model reading words with the *igh* pattern, guide students to read the words, and then have students model reading the words independently. Follow up by giving students opportunities to read connected text containing words with the same spelling pattern.

These two teaching approaches can have positive effects on students' fluency. However, the best result comes from lots of practice. Here are some ideas.

Practice

There is a large body of research indicating that when students are given opportunities to practice oral reading of a particular text, their fluency improves dramatically (Chard et al., 2002). Two kinds of practice have been found especially effective: repeated reading of familiar text and coached reading, which is sometimes referred to as assisted reading.

Repeated Reading of Familiar Text Repeated oral reading has been shown to improve the fluency in students of all ages (Carver & Hoffman, 1981; O'Shea, Sindelar, & O'Shea, 1987). As students reread familiar material they get better at it, which probably comes as no surprise. And the increased exposure to the words they are reading elevates them from words students need to decode to words they can recognize by sight. Here's a procedure for repeated reading:

1. Identify text in which your student can accurately read 95–100 percent of the words orally, the student's independent level. It is best to select text that does not include a lot of proper nouns, dates, or numbers. Your purpose is to give the student multiple exposures to words he can already read.

2. Choose a regular time in the school day for repeated reading, for example, five to ten minutes during independent reading. The activity should occur on a daily basis, with the support of:

- you,

- an instructional assistant,

- an older student,

- a parent, or

- a tape recording followed by practice with a peer.

3. Determine how many times to have the student read the text you chose. A few studies have shown that reading the same text more than three times has little benefit (O'Shea et al., 1987).

4. Have the student read the passage. We recommend scheduling repeated readings so that students read the text at least three times with a combination of the individuals listed above. For example, you may have a student listen to a taped reading of a passage and then read it aloud to an older student. Then, you may have the student read the passage to you. Finally, you may have the

Cross-age tutoring can help struggling readers build fluency.

student take the passage home and read it to a parent or sibling. You might also have the student read it to you the next day as an informal assessment.

When planning the sequence of readings, be sure to schedule someone at the start who can provide corrective feedback if necessary—so it may not be a good idea, for example, to assign a peer. If the child miscues, the person reading with him might ask him to reread a section or look at the beginning of the word missed.

During daily free-reading time, you may find most struggling readers choosing books they have already read many times. Resist interfering when this happens—rereading very familiar books makes children feel successful.

Coached Reading If the text you use for fluency practice is not at the student's independent level, we recommend *coached reading* or, as it's sometimes known, *assisted reading*. Most researchers agree that accuracy alone is insufficient for fluency. Students also need to read rapidly to understand the connections between ideas in print (Nathan & Stanovich, 1991). You need to control the difficulty of the text and provide corrective feedback when a student miscues. Move students into increasingly difficult text as you continue to provide this feedback.

Coached reading is similar to guided reading. The teacher works with a small group of children for about ten minutes, using a text that is at the children's instructional level. Sometimes the children read chorally, meaning they read the text aloud simultaneously while the teacher listens and provides feedback. Alternatively, the children can "whisper read" simultaneously, with the teacher leaning in to listen to one child at a time. Both of these methods allow the teacher to hear individual children read aloud and to provide feedback. During a coached reading session, the teacher guides children to select the appropriate decoding strategy for dealing with an unknown word. She also might prompt comprehension by asking meaningful questions about plot or characters. Once you've used a text for coached reading, use it for repeated reading to provide students with extra practice if they need it.

Fluency components embedded in a program of instruction provide students with opportunities to read widely (see the next section for more about wide reading) in progressively more difficult text with corrective feedback (Kuhn & Stahl, 2000). We caution, however, that using fluency-building activities before a student has sufficient phonics knowledge, high-frequency words, and a reliable decoding strategy can be frustrating. Therefore, the most helpful activities are based on having students read from material at their independent reading level.

Fluent reading is self-perpetuating. In other words, the more we read, the better we get. The better we get, the more we read. The benefits of reading a lot and reading widely are well documented. Both activities help students in all three components of fluency—rate, accuracy, and prosody.

Apply

Since most non-fluent readers don't enjoy reading, they don't read widely. However, the more widely students read, the more they enjoy it. Talk about a catch-22!

In her critical review of beginning reading research, Adams (1990) concluded: "If we want children to read well, we must find a way to induce them to read lots" (p. 5). "Children should be given as much opportunity and encouragement as possible to practice their reading. Beyond the basics, children's reading facility, as well as their vocabulary and conceptual growth, depends strongly on the amount of text they read" (p. 127). Wide reading has been associated with gains not only in reading fluency, but also in language and cognitive abilities (Stanovich & Cunningham, 1992). The students who need the most encouragement to read widely are the students who struggle.

Wide Reading Students are more likely to read widely and, therefore, build fluency when they are given books that are interesting to them and that don't pose word-recognition problems for them. Here are some specific ways to promote wide reading:

- Provide ample reading material that appeals to a range of interests, such as informational books (e.g., nature, travel, biography) and other genres (fantasy, poetry, plays). Have on hand magazines, comic books, directions for making things, telephone books, cookbooks, cereal boxes—anything that interests your students.

- Team with school and community libraries to improve interest in and access to books and magazines. For example, host a library night for families and encourage them to select books for members to read together or individually. At the event, demonstrate Read Aloud practices and distribute library cards.

- Encourage students to form book clubs. After several students have read the same book, encourage them to meet periodically and discuss their favorite parts, or help each other understand difficult parts. They may also talk about other books by the same author or other books on the same theme.

- Have students write scripts based on stories they have read and act them out for the class. Writing a script based on a story requires comprehension. Taking on the role of a character and saying the dialogue requires fluency.

- Ask students to write book reviews for the school newspaper. This requires students to evaluate books using some kind of criteria, such as whether the piece is well written, whether the information is helpful, or whether the story is exciting.

- Establish a link with families by sending newsletters home about the reading students are doing in school. Invite parents to respond with a letter about books children are reading at home. If you have Internet access or a school Web site, you can save trees by corresponding through e-mail or postings on the site.

Reassess

Even the most thoughtful and well-planned approach to fluency instruction may fall short of what a struggling reader needs. Therefore, it is important to monitor progress.

Monitoring a student's progress is similar to the initial assessment of fluency. However, a single reading of one passage is sufficient. The passage you choose should reflect the child's current independent reading level, so don't assume that passages you used for the initial assessment will work for monitoring. Presumably (and hopefully), the child's fluency has increased and, therefore, so should the level of text you use.

For most readers in the elementary grades, we recommend formal monitoring of fluency three times per year. However, for struggling readers we recommend at least once per week. The more frequently you measure progress, the more confidence you have in your data.

Once you've selected the passages, establish a goal for fluency development by taking the student's current fluency in CWPM and estimating the number of words-per-week growth you expect. Fuchs, Fuchs, Hamlett, Walz, and Germann (1993) estimated that in first and second grades, students working on fluency building should be able to gain two words per week. So, a student reading 35 CWPM should be reading approximately 55 CWPM after ten weeks of working on fluency. Fuchs et al. (1993) found that for students in third grade and higher, per-week growth estimates were slightly lower, approximately one word. These estimated growth rates allow us to set specific goals for fluency growth and to determine whether or not our fluency intervention is successful. Creating a graph like the one in Figure 6.4 allows you to show progress over time.

The goal line is based on the growth estimates we described earlier. The CWPM line represents the student's actual reading fluency. Overall, the student's growth mirrors the goal line. This is a good sign. If the student's actual growth was either far above the goal line or far below it, adjustments to instruction and assessment would need to be made. If a student's growth is better than expected, he or she may not need further fluency intervention. If the student's growth is lagging, reevaluate your diagnosis, reconsider the procedures you have been using for fluency training, and try an alternative.

Don't forget to note improvements in prosody, or "reading with expression," along with rate and accuracy. After all, a student's attention to prosody is an indication of his understanding of the text he is reading.

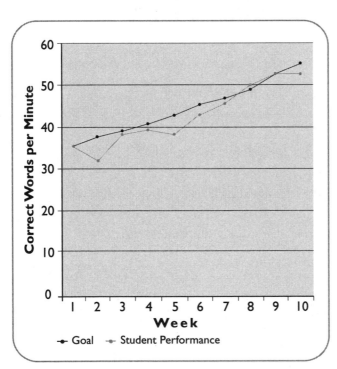

FIGURE 6.4 Sample progress monitoring for one child

Sample Teach and/or Practice Steps Using the Intervention Framework

At the beginning of the chapter, we saw three kinds of fluency problems in Ms. Gomez's students:

- Elisha, Jamal, and Caitlin's rates and accuracy were below grade level.

- Natalie's rate and accuracy were okay, but her prosody was not.

- Will and Sandra made frequent substitutions and did not use knowledge of word types.

The same initial assessment and diagnosis, application, and final assessment were used for these six students. However, Ms. Gomez's teaching and the practice opportunities she provided varied based on the individual needs. Here's an overview of how she helped all six students:

- **Fluency Characteristic:** *Slow Reading* Elisha, Jamal, and Caitlin need to increase their reading rate. Intervention for them focuses on practice: repeated reading of familiar text to build rate.

- **Fluency Characteristic:** *Poor Use of Expression or Attention to Prosody* Natalie read at the appropriate rate and accuracy for her grade. However, she seldom paid attention to text features such as punctuation. Her oral reading was flat and without expression. When she was asked questions about what she had just read aloud, she was unable to provide answers, suggesting that she paid little attention to meaning as she read.

Teach/Reteach

Natalie would benefit from modeled reading, which is described on page 108. Begin by reading aloud an independent-level passage to Natalie as she reads along silently, having her focus primarily on the content. Immediately after you model, have her read the same passage orally. If she still reads with poor expression, repeat the procedure, calling attention to the features that help you read with expression. It may also be helpful to model reading the same passage without expression and then with expression. With each model reading, release to Natalie responsibility for noticing features.

Once Natalie can read passages well with your help, consider giving her passages on tape to imitate for practice. Once she's mastered those passages, she should be able to read new material on her own, with expression.

Students select books to take home to read aloud to their families.

Practice

Natalie might benefit from practicing reading aloud a story on her own and then reading it aloud to younger children. Having an audience stimulates reading with expression. Preparation for reading aloud to a younger child would give her a purpose for repeated oral reading.

Encourage repeated reading of familiar text at home. Send a letter to Natalie's family suggesting ways it can support good oral reading by modeling. By reading aloud together with a family member, Natalie will continue to build her ability to read with expression.

- **Fluency Characteristic:** *Repeated Misreading of Particular Words or Word Types* Will and Sandra make frequent substitutions and errors of certain word types. They need direct teaching to help them overcome these impediments to fluent reading.

Example 1

Teach Will and Sandra to decode the words that are giving them trouble, by blending sounds from left to right—saying each sound in order and then saying the word fast, as described earlier. Students who substitute one word for another may not be paying attention to the beginnings of words. To help them, model

The Struggling Reader: Interventions That Work

sequential decoding of words by displaying words individually, sounding out each phoneme, and then saying the word fast.

Will and Sandra may need many sessions devoted to blending. While it may also be helpful to have them think about how a substituted word usually doesn't make sense in the passage, it will probably be more helpful to get them to pay attention to the beginning sounds in the words and apply the blending strategy automatically.

Practice

Level 1 Will and Sandra should receive coached reading so that you can catch substitutions and remind them to use what they have just learned about noting the beginnings of words and decoding sounds in sequence.

Level 2 Will and Sandra should do repeated readings of text they have just read with your coaching.

Example 2

Will and Sandra also had problems reading words with the *eigh* pattern. Use explicit teaching of the phoneme/grapheme (sound/symbol). (See Chapter 4 on teaching word recognition.) Provide examples of words with the pattern they do not recognize: *eight, freight, weight, neighbor, weigh.*

Practice

First, provide coached reading of text that contains words with the target pattern. Then, carry out repeated readings of the same text.

Conclusion

Fluency can be a serious problem for many struggling readers. There is a strong research and theoretical base that indicates that fluency is absolutely necessary for comprehension. If a reader has not developed fluency, the process of decoding words pulls attention away from constructing meaning. Substantial research has also been conducted on how to develop fluency. When teachers like Ms. Gomez carefully diagnose students' fluency needs and match them with research-based approaches to improving fluency, such as those presented in this chapter, students read with increasing ease and understanding.

CHAPTER 7

Comprehension

CASE STUDY

It is the beginning of the school year. Sixth-grade teacher Brenda Soto has asked a group of eight students to read silently an excerpt from *Hatchet* by Gary Paulsen, which is part of a commercial literature anthology for sixth graders. She is trying to find out how well her students read and understand the grade-level text. She introduces the selection with a group discussion and then has students read a passage to determine how Brian, the main character whose small plane crashes in the wilderness, handles being alone. Then she has students work with partners to develop oral summaries of the passage.

Brenda immediately notices that three students are experiencing real difficulties accomplishing the assignment. She sits with one student, Anita, and asks her to read aloud the part that tells how Brian behaved in the wilderness. Anita cannot retell what she has read. In fact, she is unable to read aloud many of the words.

Brenda moves on to Kenny and asks him to read aloud the same part. Unlike Anita, Kenny reads aloud every word perfectly, but like Anita cannot retell any of the key points. It is obvious that he has failed to comprehend the text.

Brenda moves on to Terry and asks her to tell what she has learned from her reading. Terry is unable to summarize key points even as she examines the text in an attempt to do so.

The group comes together for a discussion. Five students seem to have read and understood the selection very well. They summarize how Brian was able to build a fire. However, the three students who met individually with Brenda were unable to contribute because they either could not read the text or did not understand its ideas.

Brenda Soto clearly has students who are struggling with reading. For Anita, the text was probably too difficult, considering the extent to which she struggled with its words. Although Kenny could recognize the words, he was still unable to comprehend the text most likely because he lacks the needed background or does not know how to use comprehension strategies. Terry was not able to comprehend the text either, but, unlike Anita and Kenny, the source of her problem is not as clear. Brenda needs to learn more about her struggling readers' comprehension difficulties before she can help them.

In this chapter, we examine comprehension and the key comprehension strategies readers need. Then we show you through a sample lesson how to apply the intervention framework to the area of comprehension. Finally, we present two procedures for helping students apply newly acquired skills as they read extended text: a text-reading framework for struggling readers and reciprocal teaching.

Why Do Some Readers Struggle With Comprehension?

Comprehension is the process of constructing meaning by interacting with text (Anderson & Pearson, 1984). It is the primary reason one reads—to understand what has been read, not just call the words. Answering the question "Why do some readers struggle with comprehension?" is not simple. Brenda will need to think about a variety of factors to determine how to help her three struggling readers, which we explain next.

Word Recognition and/or Fluency

To comprehend a text, readers must be able to decode words quickly, easily, and automatically (National Reading Panel, 2000) and read smoothly. Readers who lack word-recognition skills and fluency often have difficulties with comprehension. Take Charles, a former fifth-grade student of ours, for example. He struggled so much with decoding, and devoted so much attention to figuring out words, that he was not able to develop adequate fluency and, therefore, comprehend effectively. However, once Charles learned decoding skills, he became a more fluent reader and was able to learn the strategies needed to comprehend. In Chapter 4, we address ways to help students having difficulty learning to decode. In Chapter 6, we focus on how to help struggling readers develop fluency.

Oral Language

Readers who have limited oral language often encounter difficulties with comprehension (Cooper & Kiger, 2005). Sometimes those limitations are related to the extent to which readers use oral language, sometimes they're related to the size and sophistication of their oral vocabulary, and sometimes they're related to both factors. Beth and Jorge were students we had in an elementary school. While they could express themselves pretty well talking with friends, they lacked many concepts about the world, and words that were common to most other students were not in their vocabularies. They also had difficulty understanding and using instructional language or school language, which made it difficult for them to carry out tasks such as following oral or written directions. As we stress in Chapter 2, oral language is the foundation for all aspects of learning to read. Refer to that chapter for a variety of ways to help students with limited oral language.

Meaning Vocabulary

Sometimes readers have comprehension difficulties because they have limited meaning vocabularies or understandings of words (Nagy, 1988). Andrea, a third-grade struggling reader, knew how to decode and read fluently. She could often pronounce the words accurately, but she frequently did not know their meanings. In Chapter 5, we show you how to help struggling readers improve their meaning vocabularies.

Prior Knowledge and Concepts

Prior knowledge includes the vocabulary, ideas, and concepts a student has, related to a particular topic. It is the foundation of reading comprehension because without sufficient existing knowledge on a topic, readers have nothing to which to apply new knowledge (Alexander & Jetton, 2000). Sometimes prior knowledge is also referred to as background knowledge. Ray was a seventh grader who had lived his entire life on a small Midwestern farm. So when his teacher gave him an article to read on life in Mexico, he could not comprehend it because he had never been out of his county, hadn't read other things about Mexico or seen movies set there, and wasn't even sure if it was another country. In other words, he had no background—or prior knowledge—related to the topic. And Ray's struggles weren't just related to Mexico—he often lacked the prior knowledge necessary to comprehend texts on many different topics. If a student has limited or inaccurate prior knowledge or concepts, he or she may have problems with comprehension. We focus on this limitation later in the chapter.

Interests and Motivation

A lack of interest in reading and/or motivation to read may also influence a student's ability to comprehend. It is hard to tell whether lack of interest and poor motivation are the result of being a struggling reader or the cause of being one. We know, though, that many upper-grade students become interested and motivated once they become successful at reading. In some cases, interest and motivation are related to specific topics. For example, Mark, a struggling fourth grader, always read better and more enthusiastically when he was reading about nature or science.

Text Factors

The characteristics of the text a student is reading—including the amount of text on the page, the difficulty of the text, and the type of text—can also influence his or her ability to comprehend (Alexander & Jetton, 2000).

When Sara, a third-grade student, was given a full page of text with no illustrations, she was overwhelmed by it; she could not pronounce the words accurately and was unable to comprehend the text. When she was given the same material spread over more pages, with less text on each page and with some illustrations, she could read the words and comprehend the text.

The difficulty of the text can also affect how well a student comprehends it. Recall Anita from Brenda Soto's class; she was unable to comprehend the grade-level anthology passage because it was too difficult for her. It is important to know the student's reading level so that you can select appropriate text. Determining reading levels is discussed in the next section.

Text type also may influence how well a student comprehends—is it narrative (story) or is it expository (informational)? Randy, a seventh-grade student, always comprehends informational text about historical subjects better than he does narrative texts or other expository texts on other topics. This is because he is familiar with the elements and structures of historical informational text, whereas he isn't familiar with the elements and structures of other text types.

Strategies

Another important variable that influences how well students comprehend is their knowledge of and ability to use *strategies* (Paris, Wasik, & Turner, 1991). Research has shown that one of the most effective ways to help students improve their comprehension is to teach them strategies (National Reading Panel, 2000). A strategy is a plan for reading a text using multiple skills. For example, summarizing is a strategy that requires the use of skills such as identifying the main idea, noting details, and sequencing. The research literature on comprehension identifies many strategies (Paris et al., 1991). Here are eight that we feel are most useful for students. Figure 7.1 explains these strategies in detail:

1. Identifying Important Information
2. Inferring/Predicting
3. Monitoring/Clarifying
4. Questioning
5. Visualizing
6. Summarizing
7. Synthesizing
8. Evaluating

In summary, struggling readers have difficulty with comprehension for a variety of reasons. To help them overcome their problems, you need to assess each student individually to determine the reason(s) for their problems and then teach them based on your findings. The next section will help you do just that.

Strategy	Definition	Comments
IDENTIFYING IMPORTANT INFORMATION	Reading a text and identifying the most important elements. In narrative texts, these are the elements of a story map (setting, characters, problem, key events, and outcome). In expository text, these are the main ideas.	This strategy is essential to knowing what the author is saying explicitly. Readers often use several strategies in combination to fully understand a text.
INFERRING/ PREDICTING	Judging, concluding, or reasoning from some given information. This can include anticipating what is going to happen or come next. This is the process of predicting.	This strategy helps students read between the lines and determine information that is not directly stated. It also helps students have a purpose for reading.
MONITORING/ CLARIFYING	Knowing whether what you are reading is making sense and having a plan to clear up your understanding if it does not make sense.	This strategy enables students do things such as reread, look at diagrams and illustrations, or think about how to figure out an unknown word.
GENERATING AND ANSWERING QUESTIONS	Posing questions before reading or during reading, which requires students to integrate information and think as they read. In addition to answering questions of their own, students also benefit from answering questions posed by the teacher and/or other students.	This strategy helps students set a purpose for their reading. When students ask questions of each other, the one asking the question must always know the answer.
VISUALIZING	Forming mental pictures in your head as you read.	This strategy is like inferential thinking in which the reader forms visuals in his/her mind as reading takes place.

(continued on the next page)

FIGURE 7.1 Key comprehension strategies

FIGURE 7.1 Key comprehension strategies *continued*

Strategy	Definition	Comments
SUMMARIZING	Pulling together the essential elements in a longer piece of text. This is like retelling in your own words.	For narrative text this strategy is focused on story elements, and for expository text it is focused on main ideas.
SYNTHESIZING	Pulling together the key ideas from several sources of information.	This strategy requires the same basic process as summarizing, except it is applied across several sources. This strategy is important as students study content areas such as science or social studies.
EVALUATING	Making judgments about what has been read.	This includes making judgments about the text, the way characters responded to certain situations, and the validity and accuracy of the content. This is the process of critical reading.

Applying the Intervention Framework to Comprehension

Recall the intervention framework that we have used throughout this book—
(1) assess and diagnose, (2) teach/reteach, (3) practice, (4) apply, and (5) reassess.
In the following sections, we show you how to use this framework to help
struggling readers improve their comprehension.

How Do You Assess and Diagnose a Struggling Reader's Comprehension?

When we analyze a student's comprehension, we consider all seven elements
discussed earlier—word recognition/fluency, oral language, meaning vocabulary,

prior knowledge/concepts, interest/motivation, text factors, and strategies and skills. We begin the assessment process by asking ourselves four questions:

1. What are the student's reading levels?

2. What is the student's listening level?

3. What types of comprehension difficulties does the student have?

4. Which key comprehension strategies is the student able to use?

This section is designed to help you address each of these questions. As you do, continually remind yourself that you are working with a struggling reader who needs specific, focused help. To provide that kind of help, make sure you have the best information possible. Don't rush to make a decision based on one mistake the student makes; rather, look for consistent patterns in the student's reading behaviors. However, once you have the information you need, stop assessing and begin teaching.

Sometimes these questions can be answered with information that you gather during the course of everyday teaching. At other times, more-detailed testing is necessary, which is the point of this section. Every struggling reader deserves to receive our best efforts in deciding what should be done to help him or her achieve maximum success in reading.

Students apply the preview strategy before reading.

What Are the Student's Reading Levels? Identifying a student's reading levels—independent, instructional, and frustration—allows you to choose the right text for instruction.

- **The independent level:** The student can read the text without any instructional support from the teacher.

- **The instructional level:** The student can read the text with support from the teacher.

- **The frustration level:** The student cannot read text even with support from the teacher.

These levels were identified by Betts (1946) many years ago and are still relied upon today by reading professionals. Figure 7.2 presents the criteria for determining reading levels, based on a student's reading of a series of passages that gradually increase in difficulty. We have also included a more recent revision of the criteria by Burns and Roe, which reflects more recent thinking about reading levels.

There are two ways to gather the information needed to determine a student's reading levels: by giving an *informal reading inventory* or informally during daily teaching.

	Word Recognition		Comprehension
Original Betts Criteria			
Independent	99%+	and	90%+
Instructional	95%+	and	75%+
Frustration	Less than 90%	or	Less than 50%
Revised Criteria Burns & Roe, 2002			
Independent	99% or higher	and	90% or higher
Instructional Grades 1–2	85% or higher	and	75% or higher
Grades 3–12	95% or higher	and	75% or higher
Frustration Grades 1–2	Below 85%	or	Below 50%
Grades 3–12	Below 90%	or	Below 50%

FIGURE 7.2 Informal reading inventory criteria

- **Determining Reading Levels Using an Informal Reading Inventory** An *informal reading inventory* (IRI) is a series of passages that are arranged in order of difficulty, from easy to more complex, and accompanying questions of different types, such as literal, inferential, critical, and vocabulary. The passages are presented in a standard form and are used by all or many of the teachers in a school. Some school districts construct their own IRIs. There are also many published informal reading inventories on the market. Here are a few of the more widely used ones:

  - *Burns/Roe Informal Reading Inventory* (preprimer to twelfth grade) Sixth Edition (revised by B. D. Roe) by P. C. Burns and B. D. Roe

  - *Basic Reading Inventory* (preprimer through grade twelve and early literacy assessments) Eighth Edition by J. L. Johns

  - *Qualitative Reading Inventory* 3 (emergent through high school) by L. Leslie and J. Caldwell

  If you are unfamiliar with administering informal reading inventories, we suggest that you refer to *Literacy Assessment: Helping Teachers Plan Instruction*, Second Edition, Chapter 10, "Measuring and Matching Readers and Materials" (Cooper & Kiger, 2005). All published IRIs also have extensive instructions to help you administer them.

  Carrying out an IRI is time-consuming but it is well worth the time because you find out so much about the needs of your struggling reader's decoding, comprehension, and overall thinking about reading, in addition to the level of text they need for instruction. IRIs also help you address the student's listening level and gives you information for analyzing specific comprehension needs such as making inferences.

- **Determining Reading Levels During Daily Teaching** At the beginning of the year or whenever you have a new student who is struggling, use your daily teaching time to gather information about reading levels. Here's how:

  1. Obtain three or four pieces of text that range in difficulty from very easy to approximately one year below the student's grade level. Text may come from graded anthologies, basal readers, or any other graded book source. Select both narrative and expository texts. Because students in upper elementary, middle, and high school are expected to comprehend both types of texts in language arts and content area studies, use examples of

Resources for Taking Retellings

If you are unfamiliar with the procedures for taking a retelling, check out the following resources:

Literacy: Helping Children Construct Meaning, Sixth Edition, Chapter 11, "Assessment and Evaluation in the Comprehensive Literacy Classroom" by J. D. Cooper with N. D. Kiger

Literacy Assessment: Helping Teachers Plan Instruction, Second Edition, Chapter 10, "Measuring and Matching Readers and Materials" by J. D. Cooper and N. D. Kiger

Basic Reading Inventory (preprimer through grade twelve and early literacy assessments), Eighth Edition, by J. L. Johns

both and compare results in order to determine reading levels for struggling readers. Follow these guidelines for the length of each piece:

- Preprimer to Primer: 25–35 words
- First and Second Grades: 40–75 words
- Third to Sixth Grades: 100–150 words
- Seventh to Twelfth Grades: 150–200 words

2. Familiarize yourself with the content.

3. Have the student sit alongside you in a quiet space and tell him that you'll be asking him to read short passages silently and, once he's finished, retell them to you. Begin with the easiest level and have the student read as many passages as needed to determine the student's three reading levels.

4. Use forms like the retelling protocols presented in Figures 7.3 and 7.4 to record the student's retelling. Make statements such as "Tell me more." and "Can you remember anything else?" to prompt the student when his retelling is not complete.

5. To determine a reading level, make a judgment call as to whether the retelling is:

- Excellent (Independent Level: almost 100% accuracy)
- Satisfactory (Instructional Level: 50%+ accuracy)
- Unsatisfactory (Frustration: 25% or less accuracy)

These criteria are based on the work of Jerry Johns (2001).

While this procedure allows you to work assessment directly into your daily teaching, it is best used as a way to monitor progress after you have initially assessed the student's needs. For this reason, we recommend using an informal reading inventory for the initial assessment of the struggling reader's reading levels.

Story Retelling Summary Sheet

Name_____ Date _____

Title _____

Student selected _____ Teacher selected _____

	SCORES	
	Unprompted	Prompted
Setting:		
Begins with introduction (1 pt.)	_____	_____
Gives time and place (1 pt.)	_____	_____
Characters:		
Names main character (1 pt.)	_____	_____
Identifies other characters (1 pt.)	_____	_____
Gives names _____		
Gives number _____		
Actual number _____		
Number given _____		
Problem:		
Identifies primary story problem (1 pt.)	_____	_____
Action:		
Recalls major events (1 pt.)	_____	_____
Outcome:		
Identifies how problem was solved (1 pt.)	_____	_____
Gives story ending (1 pt.)	_____	_____
Sequence:		
Retells story in order (2 pts. = correct; 1 pt. = partial; 0 = no evidence of sequence)	_____	_____
TOTAL SCORE (10 pts. possible)	_____	_____

Observations/comments:

Analysis:

Source: Adapted from L. M. Morrow, Using story retelling to develop comprehension, in K. D. Muth, ed., *Children's comprehension of text: Research into practice*, pp. 37–58. Copyright © 1989 International Reading Association.

FIGURE 7.3 Retelling protocol for narrative text

Informational Text Retelling Summary Sheet

Name_____ Date _____

Title _____

Student selected _____ Teacher selected _____

	SCORES	
	Unprompted	Prompted
Introduction:		
Identifies topic (1 pt.)	_____	_____
Gives some purpose or focus (1 pt.)	_____	_____
Main Ideas:	_____	_____
Number given _____		
Actual number _____		
(6 pts. = all correct; 4 pts. = $2/3$ correct; 2 pts. = $1/3$ correct; 0 pts. = none correct)		
Shows logical understanding of how ideas are related; explains ideas	_____	_____
(2 pts. = relates all ideas; 1 pt. = relates some ideas; 0 pts. = shows no relationship of ideas)		
TOTAL SCORE (10 pts. possible)	_____	_____

Observations/comments:

Analysis:

Source: Adapted from L. M. Morrow, Using story retelling to develop comprehension, in K. D. Muth, ed., *Children's comprehension of text: Research into practice*, pp. 37–58. Copyright © 1989 International Reading Association.

FIGURE 7.4 Retelling protocol for expository text

A student answers questions after listening to a passage read by the teacher for a listening test.

What Is the Student's Listening Level? A student's ability to listen to and comprehend text is a rough indicator of his or her potential or capacity to learn to read and comprehend text (Betts, 1946; Johns, 2001). We determine a student's listening level by using an alternate set of graded or leveled passages from an IRI. We read aloud passages to the student and then the student answers the accompanying questions. The highest-level passage about which the student can accurately answer 75 percent or more of the questions is considered the student's listening level.

Basic Procedures for Administering the Listening Test

1. Start with a passage one level below the student's instructional reading level. If you do not have the student's instructional reading level, determine it using the guidelines in the previous section or begin with a passage one grade level below the student's grade level.

2. Read aloud the passage and ask the student the questions. Continue reading passages in order of difficulty until the student gets fewer than 75 percent of the questions correct.

3. If a student gets fewer than 75 percent correct on the first passage, drop down to the next-lower passage. Continue with lower-level passages until you reach a point at which the student comprehends 75 percent or more of the questions.

Let's look at how we use this information to help us understand a student's comprehension needs. Adriene, a fifth grader, got the following reading scores on the IRI:

> Independent: Level 2
>
> Instructional: Levels 3–4
>
> Frustration: Level 5

Level 6 was the highest level passage on which Adriene scored 75 percent on listening. By comparing Adriene's instructional reading level (3–4) with his listening level (6), we can see that his listening level is higher. This may indicate that he has the potential to improve his reading to the same level, with the right intervention.

What Types of Comprehension Difficulties Does the Student Have? After we have determined reading levels and listening level, we analyze the student's specific comprehension needs. To do that, we examine the types of questions the student answered correctly and incorrectly. We are cautious, though; one or two mistakes on an IRI seldom are sufficient evidence to draw a conclusion about a student's overall needs. Instead, we look for a pattern of mistakes—that is, at least three or more errors on a particular question category. For example, we know that Adriene's instructional reading level is third to fourth grade. We analyzed Adriene's answers to the different types of questions on passages through his highest instructional level. This is what we found:

> Literal questions: 50% correct
>
> Inferential questions: 20% correct
>
> Critical questions: 20% correct
>
> Vocabulary questions: 90% correct

We then compared these results to the types of questions Adriene answered correctly through Level 6 on the listening assessment:

Literal questions: 100% correct

Inferential questions: 75% correct

Critical questions: 50% correct

Vocabulary questions: 100% correct

We can see that Adriene's strongest area is vocabulary in both reading and listening. In reading, his literal, inferential, and critical comprehension are generally weak, with the exception of literal comprehension at the listening level. Since his literal comprehension is so much stronger at the listening level, he may be having a problem with word recognition, so we will check that out to be sure before we begin instruction. Since Adriene's weakest areas in reading were in literal, inferential, and critical questions, we can see that he probably needs strategy instruction. We will want to check him using some of the assessment activities for checking strategy use discussed in the next section.

Which Key Comprehension Strategies Is the Student Able to Use?

Next, we look at how students use the eight major comprehension strategies that we identify in Figure 7.1. We have found the most effective way to do this is with a short reading experience in which we present the strategy to the student and see how well she is able to use it. A sample assessment for Inferencing/Predicting follows. (Inferencing and predicting are presented together because predicting relies on inference.) Use it as a basis to check the other strategies students need in order to comprehend effectively. Keep in mind that these are activities designed for checking strategy use and not for teaching strategy use, and therefore you should provide the student no assistance, so that you can get an accurate measure of his or her abilities. This procedure may be used with students at any grade level.

Assessment Activity for Checking Inferencing/Predicting

MATERIALS: a piece of narrative text and a piece of expository text at the student's instructional level, each between five and seven pages.

STRATEGY: Inferencing/Predicting

PROCEDURES:

1. Show the student one of the texts that you chose. Read the title aloud.

2. Ask the student to look at photos and illustrations and to make inferences about what is going to happen in or be learned from this text. If there are no photos or illustrations, have the student read the first and last paragraphs aloud and tell you her prediction.

3. Have the student write the predictions or write them for her.

4. Have the student read the complete text silently to see if her predictions are accurate. (If the student has not yet learned to read silently, allow her to read the text orally.)

5. After the reading, discuss whether the student was able to confirm her predictions. If she was able to do so, ask her to point out information from the text that allowed for that. If she was not able to, ask her whether she thinks the predictions might be verified later if there were more to the story. Ask her whether new predictions should be made in light of the information gained.

6. Ask the student to discuss how the strategy was helpful in reading the text.

7. Repeat the procedure with the second piece of text.

ANALYSIS:

As you conduct this assessment activity, ask yourself the following questions:

1. Is the student able to make predictions that are logical?

2. Can the student recognize that the prediction was/was not confirmed?

3. Does the student understand that as she gains information through reading new predictions can be made?

4. Is the student able to make new or additional predictions?

5. Does the student recognize how predicting helps with reading?

COMMENTS:

Observing the student's use of a strategy is the best way to determine whether the student can use the strategy effectively and which comprehension strategies should be taught.

Checking activities can focus on more than one strategy at the same time. For example, you can combine the inferencing/predicting strategy with summarizing by having students summarize what they read after checking their predictions, noting how well each student was able to summarize. It is best to focus on no more than two strategies at a time so that you don't overwhelm the student and she can concentrate on what she is doing.

Analyzing a Student's Overall Comprehension Once we have gathered the information needed to understand each student's reading levels, listening level, and use of individual comprehension strategies, we need to summarize it in a form that makes it usable to make instructional decisions. Figure 7.5 on page 137 presents a blank form that helps do this. Note that it contains spaces to summarize information about all the major areas that influence a student's comprehension that we have discussed thus far.

Now study the completed form in Figure 7.6 on page 138 for Cheryl, a fourth grader. In the discussion that follows, we share the thinking that we went into deciding how to help Cheryl improve her comprehension.

Discussion:

- Cheryl's listening level is much higher than her instructional reading level. This suggests that she has the potential to make great strides in comprehension because she already comprehends well when not faced with print.

- Since Cheryl's instructional reading level is a range of grades 2–3, we would give her second-grade texts for strategy teaching and practice. As she becomes comfortable in applying strategies, we would move her gradually to more difficult texts.

- Cheryl's word recognition, fluency, and oral language are satisfactory, which should be an asset in improving her comprehension.

- Our primary instructional focus will be on teaching the strategies of monitor/clarify, summarize, and synthesize. We will use the intervention model presented throughout this book.

- Our second focus will be on having Cheryl read texts under our direction, giving her many opportunities to apply the new strategies she's learning, as well as those she seems to know how to use—inferencing/predicting, questioning, visualizing, and noting important information. Even though she knows how to use these strategies, more opportunities for applying them and more teacher modeling of them will help as we expand the types of texts Cheryl is reading.

Comprehension Analysis Form

Name_____ Grade _____

Teacher_____ Age _____ Date _____

READING LEVELS: LISTENING LEVEL:

Independent _____   Instructional _____   Frustration _____   _____

COMMENTS:

FACTORS	SATISFACTORY	NEEDS IMPROVEMENT	COMMENTS
Word Recognition			
Fluency			
Oral Language			
Meaning Vocabulary			
Prior Knowledge/Concepts			
Interests/Motivation			
Text Factors			
Strategies: Identifying Important Information Inferencing/Predicting Monitoring/Clarifying Questioning Visualizing Summarizing Synthesizing			

INSTRUCTIONAL PLANS

Level of Text _____

Areas for Concentration:

FIGURE 7.5: Sample comprehension analysis form

Comprehension Analysis Form

Name Cheryl Jefferson   Grade 4

Teacher Mr. Stephenson   Age 10   Date 9/16

READING LEVELS: **LISTENING LEVEL:**

Independent 1   Instructional 2-3   Frustration 4   7

COMMENTS: Listening comprehension 4–5 levels higher than reading. Should be able to improve with appropriate instruction.

FACTORS	SATISFACTORY	NEEDS IMPROVEMENT	COMMENTS
Word Recognition	X		Excellent decoding skills. Can pronounce two- and three-syllable words.
Fluency	X		Accurate reading of words is excellent for grade level but does not comprehend what is read.
Oral Language	X		Appears to have good oral language. Expresses self clearly. Good oral vocabulary.
Meaning Vocabulary		X	Even though has good oral language, there are often terms she is unfamiliar with.
Prior Knowledge/Concepts		X	Excellent decoding skills. Can pronounce two- and three-syllable words.
Interests/Motivation		X	Motivation is very low. At this time, shows no real interest in any given topic except reading mysteries.
Text Factors	X		Reads and comprehends much better in narrative text than in expository.
Strategies: Identifying Important Information Inferencing/Predicting Monitoring/Clarifying Questioning Visualizing Summarizing Synthesizing	X X X X	 X X X	Uses all strategies. Better in narrative text than in expository text. Needs work with monitor/clarify, summarize, and synthesize with both types of texts.

INSTRUCTIONAL PLANS

Level of Text 2

Areas for Concentration:

1. Modeling strategies—monitor/clarify, summarize, and synthesize.
2. Focus an application and use of all strategies.
3. Select text of interest (mysteries). Expand expository interests.
4. Text reading using the text reading framework presented in this chapter. Emphasize prior knowledge, concepts, and vocabulary.

FIGURE 7.6 Completed comprehension analysis form

- For all text reading, we will start with many short stories and mystery books since Cheryl enjoys that genre. As she gains confidence, we will move her into other types of narrative texts and into expository or informational texts. Once Cheryl is reading a variety of texts, we will concentrate on building her meaning vocabulary, prior knowledge, and concepts. We will also teach her to apply strategies in various types of text.

- At least once a month, we will use the retelling procedures described earlier in Figures 7.3 and 7.4 to monitor Cheryl's comprehension growth in both narrative and expository texts. We will monitor her use of the strategies by observing her closely during reading time.

We now have a good basis to begin Cheryl's comprehension instruction. Once we begin that instruction, we will constantly monitor her progress and change our plans as necessary.

Thorough analysis of each struggling reader's needs is essential to planning effective instruction. Let's look at some examples of effective instruction to consider for helping struggling readers overcome difficulties in comprehension.

Developing and Teaching Comprehension Strategy Lessons Following the Intervention Framework

We use assessment data to plan and carry out instruction along two lines:

- We provide direct instruction in the strategies the student struggles with most, by continuing to use the intervention framework that we introduced in Chapter 1, beyond the assess and diagnose stage: teach/reteach, practice, apply, and reassess.

- We provide many opportunities for the student to apply all strategies—the ones he's learning as well as the ones he's mastered—in texts that interest him and that he can read independently.

In this section, we look at these two components in depth, continuing to follow Cheryl's progress.

Our assessment and diagnosis for Cheryl indicates that she needs instruction in the strategy of summarizing. (See discussion, pages 140–145.) Since she is more comfortable with narrative texts, especially mysteries, we use this type of text for instruction, especially when she is applying the strategy on her own. If there are other students in the class who are struggling with summarizing, we create a small group for instruction. We develop all strategy lessons by continuing to apply the intervention framework. Here's how:

Teach/Reteach

To teach the strategy of summarizing, we explain the concept of summarizing and model the strategy first at the listening level and then at the reading level as described in the next section. All three of these steps—explaining the concept, modeling at the listening level, and modeling at the reading level—are especially necessary for struggling readers because they frequently fail to develop the use of strategies at all three levels.

Explaining the Concept of Summarizing

1. Start by saying to students, "You are going to learn a strategy, or plan, called summarizing to help you understand and remember what you read."

2. Tell students, "Think about one of your favorite television cartoons or movies." Then ask them to tell you the main points of the cartoon or movie in one or two sentences. Students may give you a one-word response or, on the other hand, tell every detail.

3. After students share, select a favorite cartoon or movie of your own and give a one- or two-sentence summary. For example, using the movie *Cinderella*, you might say, "This is a story about a young girl, Cinderella, her two step-sisters and her wicked stepmother. In the end Cinderella is found by the Prince and lives happily ever after."

4. Tell students that what you did was summarize. Ask students, "Did I tell everything about the movie? No, I told only the most important information or details in my own words." Guide students to compare their summaries with yours.

Modeling the Strategy at the Listening Level

1. Introduce the strategy poster for summarizing in Figure 7.7. Lead students in a discussion of each of the four steps.

Summarizing Stories
(Narrative Text)

1. Read your story to find the important parts:
   - Setting
   - Characters
   - Problem
   - Action
   - Outcome

   Make notes.

2. Look over your notes and decide what can be left out.

First I will tell the title and the author. Then, I'll tell...

3. Think about how you will tell or write your summary to make it clear.

4. Tell or write your summary.

FIGURE 7.7 Strategy poster for summarizing stories

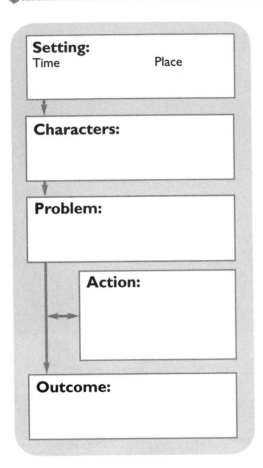

FIGURE 7.8 Sample story map

2. Display a story map like the one shown in Figure 7.8. Tell students that when they summarize stories, they need to remember characters, setting, problem, action, and outcome. Discuss the meaning of each of those elements.

3. Tell students that you are going to read aloud several paragraphs from a book, such as *Encyclopedia Brown Tracks Them Down* (Sobol, 1971). Ask them to listen for and think about elements from the story map as you read.

4. After reading aloud the paragraphs, demonstrate how to summarize them orally. Point to elements on the story map, telling students why you included each one in your summary. Students can later use the map to guide their written summaries. When doing this with struggling readers, you will most likely need to repeat this step several times using different text samples.

5. Tell students to listen to the next three or four paragraphs and summarize them following the story map, as you did.

6. Guide students to summarize verbally what they have learned about summarizing stories. This process is frequently difficult for struggling readers and requires multiple attempts with repeated teacher modeling (Vaughn, Gersten, & Chard, 2000). Use statements like these to prompt students:

   • What did we follow to guide us in summarizing parts of this story? (story map)

   • Whose words did we use to retell the story? (our own) How much of the story did we tell? (only the important parts)

The Struggling Reader: Interventions That Work

Modeling the Strategy at the Reading Level

1. Make sure each student has a copy of the book and say, "As we read the next two pages of *Encyclopedia Brown Tracks Them Down*, you're going to learn to summarize what you read. Read pages 4 and 5 to yourself while I read them aloud. When we finish, I will model how to summarize this part of our story by thinking aloud. Remember to think about the elements on the story map."

2. After reading, think aloud for the students along these lines: "Our characters are still Leroy and the ambassador. The problem is that the ambassador is missing. It looks like Leroy is going to solve the case by using clues from the gifts brought to the birthday party. We will have to read the final section to see how the case ends."

3. Tell students that you want them to read silently the remaining text and, when they're done, give you a summary. After students have completed the reading, have several of them give their models. Help them with prompts as needed, such as "Did you tell when and where the story took place?" "Did you state the problem?"

4. Conclude with a discussion about the process, bringing out the following points:

    *   What did we think about as we gave our summaries? (the story map) Why? (because we knew we were reading a story)

    *   What would we do if we didn't know for sure it was a story when we began reading? (as we read, look for characters, a problem, and so on)

    *   Whose words did we use to retell the story? (our own)

    *   How much did we include in our summary? (just the important points)

    *   How is this going to help us read? (It will help us understand the story and remember it.)

Notice that in the last two parts of the Teach step, listening and reading, we model the process for the students and then have them try immediately, or model, it themselves. Struggling readers need to immediately try what they are learning to make the process memorable.

Practice

Select a passage from a book or short story at the student's instructional level and of interest to the student. For Cheryl and students like her, we would choose a mystery at level 2, which is about eight to ten or 12 pages. Before students begin to read, introduce the text using the Text Reading Framework for Struggling Readers described later in this chapter on page 147. Then ask them to read the text silently using the strategy of summarizing. Remind students to use the strategy poster to help them remember the steps to follow.

After they've finished, have students work in partners to develop an oral summary. Have students share their summaries. Based on your observations, determine which students are still struggling (and therefore need reteaching with more teacher modeling), which ones are on their way but not quite there (and therefore need more practice), and which ones have a firm grasp of the strategy (and therefore are ready for application).

Struggling readers typically need more practice than non-struggling readers. Having students work with partners is a good way to provide that practice. When you create partnerships, vary their composition. Sometimes put two struggling

Even very young students can work in pairs to develop summaries.

readers together; pairing a struggling reader with a better reader may not be helpful because, we've found, the better reader usually does all the work. On the other hand, if you first demonstrate how partnering should work, the better reader can serve as a model for the struggling reader.

Apply

Select a short story that is at the students' instructional reading level and of interest to the group. Introduce the story using the Text Reading Framework explained on page 147. Also, remind students to use the strategy poster for summarizing to help them remember the steps they should follow. Have students read the short story silently. After they are done, have students develop oral summaries on their own to share with the group. When students are comfortable summarizing orally, teach a lesson on writing summaries. Have students share their summaries. Note how they are performing and decide who needs reteaching, more practice, or more application.

Conducting Intervention Lessons With Struggling Readers: General Guidelines

Intervention lessons for helping struggling readers improve their comprehension must be taught systematically and rigorously, in order to help students make more than adequate yearly progress and, therefore, catch up with their classmates. The following guidelines should help you:

- Teach multiple strategies a student needs to learn simultaneously. For example, Cheryl needs to learn to monitor/clarify, summarize, and synthesize. By presenting the Teach step for each of these strategies first, Cheryl can concentrate on practicing and applying all three strategies at the same time, which, of course, is the way proficient readers use strategies. This does not mean that you won't have to go back, reteach, and provide more modeling along the way. Research shows that struggling readers learn strategies effectively when they are introduced this way (Cooper, Boschken, McWilliams, & Pistochini, 2000).

- Always display a poster with the steps for or a description of using the strategy. Many teachers like to give older students a bookmark containing this information. Students keep the bookmark in their texts and refer to it while reading. See Figure 7.9 for an example.

- When teaching strategies to struggling readers, always include these three steps: explain the concept, model the strategy at the listening level, and model it at the reading level. Teacher modeling is crucial for struggling readers, moving from strong teacher support to less support to students' trying the strategies independently.

- Give struggling readers more opportunities than non-struggling readers to apply the strategies they are learning. Many of these applications should be carried out in teacher-led small groups, which make it possible for you to assess the students' progress and determine the need for additional teaching, practice, and application.

Strategies to Help Me Read...

(1) Identify Important Information

* If it is a story, think about the story map.
* If it is informational text, think about main ideas.

(2) Summarize

* Retell in my own words.

(3) Question

* Ask questions before, during, and after reading.

(4) Monitor

* Does what I am reading make sense?

(5) Predict

* What will happen?
* What will I learn?

When struggling readers are ready for more application, have them continue to use the strategy, based on individual books that you help them select. Even when some students in the group have reached this stage, you should also continue whole-group work based on a single text to allow for teacher-led discussions. Students are much more likely to continue using strategies if they can talk about them as a group. This also allows you to see how much students are learning and how well they are using the strategy.

The application stage is especially critical for helping struggling readers internalize strategies. It gives them an opportunity to use the strategy repeatedly while reading a book that is at their level and of interest to them. It is not uncommon, though, for struggling readers to require multiple reteachings, practices, and applications, so be sure to give students plenty of time to learn strategies.

FIGURE 7.9 Bookmark featuring strategies to apply before, during, and after reading

The Struggling Reader: Interventions That Work

Reassess

Ongoing observation is critical during the first four stages of the intervention framework to determine whether a student is ready to move from one stage to the next. However, once the student has had multiple opportunities to apply the strategy and you feel he or she has mastered it, do a final assessment using a Strategy Checking Activity as described on page 134 earlier in this chapter.

We can't expect students to become skilled readers only by learning strategies and applying them to passages. We must go a step further by teaching them to use all strategies automatically on a day-to-day basis, in texts that they choose and use for authentic purposes. In the following section, we present a Text Reading Framework that will put struggling readers on the road to doing just that (Cooper, 2006). Following that section, we describe reciprocal teaching, an alternative procedure that may work when the Text Reading Framework does not.

Text Reading Framework for Struggling Readers

It may seem obvious, but research shows that one of the reasons struggling readers don't read better is that they do not get to read enough either on their own or as part of teacher-directed lessons (Allington, 2001). Figure 7.10 summarizes a framework for organizing text reading for struggling readers that can be used during the Apply step of the intervention framework. Look over the table and then read the discussion about each component that follows.

This framework, similar to a Directed Reading Lesson, a Literacy Lesson (Cooper, 2006), or guided reading, gives us a structure for organizing lessons. Use it on a regular basis to help students apply comprehension strategies as well as other strategies such as decoding. Divide chosen texts into sections, or chunks, as necessary to avoid overwhelming struggling readers. Following is a discussion of each part of the Text Reading Framework.

Component	Functions	Comments
Introduce the Text	• Activate prior knowledge, concepts, and develop vocabulary. • Use predict or question.	This sets the student up to read for success by developing needed background and setting a purpose for reading.
Read the Text	• Remind students to think about what they already know, as well as their predictions or questions as they read. • Remind students to use other strategies they have learned. • Students read silently.	Reminders help keep students focused on the strategies.
Respond to the Text	• Students check predictions or answer questions. • Students and/or teacher summarize. • Group/class discusses how strategies were used and were helpful. • Extend text reading by having students write, review a skill, do vocabulary expansion activities, and so on.	Responding is a major part of the student's comprehension. Discussing the strategies helps students internalize them.

FIGURE 7.10 Text Reading Framework for teaching struggling readers

Introduce the Text

In this part of the lesson, you set students up for success by activating prior knowledge, building background, and developing key concept vocabulary. Prior knowledge or background is the information and concepts a student brings to the reading experience to comprehend a particular text. Vocabulary is a part of prior knowledge and background. It is important for these to be developed together so that students get the most out of them. In Chapter 5 we looked at a variety of ways to teach vocabulary for struggling readers. In the next section, we examine several ways to tie vocabulary, background, concepts, and prior knowledge together.

During this section of the lesson, students apply some of the strategies they have learned. Having students make predictions or pose questions about what they are going to read gives them a purpose for reading. Predictions and questions can be used for both narrative and expository texts, although posing questions is usually best for expository texts because questions help students focus on information that those texts contain.

Activating and Developing Prior Knowledge, Background, and Vocabulary Successful comprehension depends upon prior knowledge and background (Alexander & Jetton, 2000), which struggling readers frequently lack. So it makes sense to begin the experience by activating and developing those two areas. If students lack prior knowledge for a particular text, we must build the needed background to help them be successful. The more closely we connect prior knowledge, background, and vocabulary development before reading a text, the more likely we are to help the struggling reader comprehend it. Here are some guidelines:

- **Keep in mind, the goal is for struggling readers to activate their own prior knowledge when reading independently.** If a student has no prior knowledge or extremely limited prior knowledge for a piece of text, we must help develop it. As the student reads more widely, his or her prior knowledge should increase. By using various strategies that we teach, the student should be able to activate his or her own prior knowledge in order to read a text. (See Figure 7.1 for a list of key comprehension strategies.) For example, a third-grade struggling reader who knows a lot about dinosaurs is reading a book on that topic. By skimming through the text and predicting what might be learned, the student is able to activate what he knows about dinosaurs. If another student who knows very little about dinosaurs attempts to read the same book, chances are that skimming and predicting are not going to help him activate his prior knowledge as much because he has little or none to activate. Therefore, he needs teacher support to build his background knowledge about dinosaurs. As he progresses, he should gain knowledge and, by the next time he reads a book on dinosaurs, he will have some prior knowledge to activate.

- **Before students read a particular text, preview the text carefully to identify the prior knowledge needed to understand it.** The prior knowledge that is going to help any reader better comprehend a text must be directly related to that text. Therefore, be sure to read the text before students read it in order to identify the story elements (characters, setting, problem, action, and outcomes) in narrative texts and the main ideas and supporting details in expository texts. Knowing this information will help you identify the prior knowledge students need to understand the text.

   Be sure to avoid developing too much prior knowledge or the wrong prior knowledge for a piece of text. For example, if students are going to read *Potato: A Tale from the Great Depression* (Lied, 1997), they need only minimal information about the Great Depression—basically, that it was a time when people had difficulty earning money. Students do not need to know all the details about the cause of the Depression because it does not influence the understanding of the story.

- **Think about the prior knowledge and background each student already holds as it relates to the text they are going to read.** After you have identified the prior knowledge students need in order to read and understand a particular text, think about the prior knowledge of the students who are going to read it. How do the two match? Do students have some prior knowledge? Can they activate it on their own? Do they need your support? The answers to these questions will help you decide which procedures you need to carry out to prepare students for the text reading experience.

- **Use procedures that integrate prior knowledge, background, and vocabulary.** Since these three areas are related, they need to be developed together. In other words, don't use procedures that focus on prior knowledge, background, and vocabulary as separate items. Teaching lists of words in isolation is not effective in developing vocabulary and prior knowledge together, for example. Teaching vocabulary as a part of a preview of a text is effective, however. (The next section contains ideas for previewing.)

- **Keep students focused on the particular prior knowledge related to the text.** In our experience, struggling readers are known for getting the teacher off-task to delay the reading they have to do. For example, we saw a teacher who said to a group of struggling readers, "We are going to read a story about a runaway dog. Who can tell us about a dog or other pet that ran away?" The students went off on a nearly 30-minute tangent about their pets that had run away. A more effective approach would have been for the teacher to have said, "We are going to read this story about a runaway dog. Let's look at the photos and see if we can tell what we think the story is going to be about," and then browsed the book's photos with students to help them develop the background necessary to understand the story. Then she could have had the students predict what they think is going to happen in the story.

There are many effective ways to develop prior knowledge, background, and vocabulary together (Cooper, 2006) at the Introduce part of the Text Reading Framework. Let's look at one example, previewing, and its multiple variations.

Previewing *Previewing* is the process of looking through a text that is going to be read to get a general idea of what it covers. It may be done with heavy teacher support or independently by students, along a continuum made up of picture walk, guided preview, cooperative preview, independent preview, and skimming/scanning. This movement from heavy teacher support to student independence is known as *scaffolded instruction*.

- **Picture Walk** The teacher guides students through a text, using the pictures, illustrations, photographs, and/or other graphics to develop a sense of the "big picture." It can be used with students of any age or grade level as long as the text has graphic material. Here's what you do:

  1. Before working with students, read the text to familiarize yourself with the important ideas, story line, key terms, and so forth.

  2. Gather students together. If appropriate, show them the cover and have them predict what the text is likely to be about or what is going to happen, or have them pose questions that they think might be answered by the text.

  3. Browse the text with students, using the graphics as prompts to help students talk about what will happen or what they will learn. Point to key vocabulary words and briefly discuss their meanings as they come up during the discussion. Prompt students to respond by asking questions such as "What is the character in the illustration doing?" or "What can

you tell from the photograph?" The idea is to keep the students actively involved.

4. Develop a general outline for the story or information presented in the text without giving away the story ending or all details to be learned.

Picture walk gives struggling readers the needed framework to comprehend text effectively. As students become more successful with their reading, move to one of the following procedures, which require less teacher support.

- **Guided Preview** A variation of picture walk, guided preview is generally used with texts that have few graphics. Instead of showing and discussing graphics, you read aloud key sentences from the text to give students a basis for predictions and/or questions.

- **Cooperative Preview** Students work collaboratively to familiarize themselves with a text to be read, with you providing support as needed. Here's what you do:

  1. Pair up students and give partners a copy of the text to be read.

  2. Direct partners to skim pages, looking at subtitles, graphics, and captions in order to predict and question what they think they are going to learn.

  3. After a couple of minutes, ask students to share their predictions and questions with the group.

  4. Use prompts to make sure students focus on the key vocabulary. For example, if students are previewing *Mummies & Their Mysteries* (Wilcox, 1993), you might ask:

     - On page 26, find a word that means "people who look for or study something." (*researchers*)

     - Also on page 26, find a word that means "little parts and pieces." (*traces*)

     - On page 27, find a word that means "hints about something." (*clues*)

- **Independent Preview** This is very similar to the cooperative preview except that students work alone. After they preview the text, they share predictions and questions with the group. Then you focus students' attention on key vocabulary in the same way you did with the cooperative preview.

Move students as quickly as possible to independent preview to make them responsible for activating their prior knowledge.

- **Skimming/Scanning** Use this procedure after students have become successful with the procedures discussed thus far, as it requires a high level of independence. When teaching skimming/scanning, you encourage students to read over portions of a text quickly to get an idea of what they are about. Once students can do this on their own, they can assume even more responsibility for activating their prior knowledge. To get them to that point, you will need to model the process and give students ample opportunity to practice it.

Read the Text

During this part of the Text Reading Framework, students read the text and apply the strategies in a *shared reading* context, led by you. As quickly as possible, though, you should move students to silent reading. Silent reading will most likely need to be modeled by you by first giving a definition (For example, you might say: "Boys and girls, we are going to learn to read silently. When we read silently, we don't say the words aloud. We think the words in our heads.") and then demonstrating. See Chapter 4, page 59, for an example of modeling oral to silent reading.

Before students begin to read, remind them to keep in mind their predictions or questions from the Introduce step. Also, be sure to adjust the amount of text you ask students to read according to their abilities. For example, a student who is really struggling may read only a few sentences, whereas a more capable reader may be able to handle whole paragraphs. Periodically during reading, stop all students at the same place and discuss the text's content and the strategies students are using to comprehend it. Ask students to model how they use a certain strategy. If they are still having difficulty with the strategy, model it for them. Then have students continue reading and try the strategy.

Respond to the Text

The final step in the Text Reading Framework takes place after reading, when students check their predictions and answer their questions. This step is important because it puts the focus on the purpose for reading. It also allows you to see how well students are able to predict or question.

If students can confirm predictions and answer questions, see if they can summarize the text. If they have difficulty summarizing, plan to teach a lesson on it. If they don't, have them give a summary, providing models if students begin to struggle.

Post-Reading Discussions Have students engage in post-reading small-group and whole-class discussions on the important elements in the text. Discussions should be kept short, usually two or three minutes for students in the early grades and around five to ten minutes for students in the later grades. If you allow discussions to go on for too long, students get off-task. Since struggling readers often do not get the opportunity to participate in small-group discussions because more competent, more outspoken classmates overshadow them, organize the groups carefully. Try not to place struggling readers with students who might dominate them. However, groups composed only of struggling readers may not have very lengthy or sophisticated discussions.

To keep discussions moving, you may need to prompt students with relevant questions and topics. For example, the following discussion prompts might be used after reading *Encyclopedia Brown Tracks Them Down*:

- How did your predictions turn out?
- Discuss how Leroy handled the case.
- How would you have handled the case if you had been Leroy?

Prompts should always steer discussions toward predictions or questions posed before reading. They should also focus on key elements in the text to help struggling readers develop an overall picture of what they have read.

During discussions, students should remain focused on which strategies they used and how they helped them with their reading—a process that will become more natural to students as they take ownership of the strategies through practice and your careful prompting.

Graphic Organizers Another effective research-proven way to help struggling readers improve their comprehension is by having them complete graphic organizers such as the story map in Figure 7.8 (National Reading Panel, 2000). A word of caution: graphic organizers should not be required after every reading assignment because students get bored and lose interest in using them.

Extension Activities Students can also respond to the selection they have read by carrying out some kind of extension activity involving writing, art, or music. Doing a few of these activities from time to time can be motivating for students. Struggling readers enjoy the success of being able to do something with what they have read. For example, have students write a short script for a play and perform it, turn a story into a cartoon and draw the cartoon scenes, or perform an experiment after reading a science piece. Don't let the extensions become the primary focus of reading. Too often struggling readers are given activities that have little to do with improving their reading and take time away from the instruction they need.

Systematically applying the Text Reading Framework will greatly improve struggling readers' ability to apply strategies and, therefore, comprehend text. However, you may need another form of intervention when the Text Reading Framework is not effective for a particular student or group of students. In the next section, we discuss another form, Reciprocal Teaching, a research-based strategy that has been shown to improve the comprehension of struggling readers.

Reciprocal Teaching

One of the most effective procedures for helping struggling readers improve their comprehension, *reciprocal teaching* is an interactive process in which the student and teacher take turns modeling four strategies (predict, question, summarize, and clarify) after silently reading a chunk of text. The procedure was developed in the 1980s (Palincsar & Brown, 1984) as a way to accelerate the reading achievement of struggling older readers. Since then, it has also been used successfully with students at other levels to help them make more than adequate yearly progress and get them reading on level (Cooper et al., 2000; Oczkus, 2003). Our space here allows us to present only general guidelines for carrying out reciprocal teaching with struggling readers. For a more complete discussion, read *Reciprocal Teaching at Work: Strategies for Improving Reading Comprehension*, Newark, DE: International Reading Association, by Lori D. Oczkus, 2003.

1. Introduce the concept of reciprocal teaching. Explain to students that you will be taking turns "being teacher" with them and modeling four strategies that will help them better understand what they read: predict, clarify, question, and summarize. If your students are like ours, they will enjoy being told that you and they will alternate in the teacher role.

2. Introduce the four strategies by discussing clearly each one and its purpose. Display a poster like the one in Figure 7.11 to guide your discussion and help students remember the strategies. Model each strategy using a piece of very easy text. (Nursery rhymes such as "Jack and Jill" work well.) This allows students to focus on learning the strategies and not get hung up on the text.

   Introduce the text using procedures suggested earlier in this chapter for building background. After students read the text silently, model the strategies one at a time. Then have several students model the strategy. Remember, at this point, your goal is to introduce the strategies, not to have students master them. Here's an example of what modeling might look like after reading "Jack and Jill":

TEACHER: First, I am going to model summarize. What do you do when you summarize?

LARRY :   You tell what you read in your own words.

TEACHER :   How much do we tell?

LARRY: Just the important parts.

TEACHER :   My summary is, a boy and girl went up the hill to get some water and had an accident. Carol, can you give us a summary?

CAROL: Jack and Jill went up the hill to get some water and they fell down.

TEACHER :   Who would like to volunteer to give another one?

MARY ANN: Jack and Jill got hurt getting water.

TEACHER :   The next strategy I am going to model is question; I am going to ask something about the story. Who went up the hill? Terri.

TERRI: Jack and Jill.

When I read, do I...

* **summarize:** tell briefly in my own words?

* **clarify:** explain how I figured something out?

* **question:** ask something about the text?

* **predict:** tell what is likely to happen or what I will learn?

FIGURE 7.11 Reciprocal Teaching Strategies Poster

TEACHER : Terri, can you ask a question and call on someone to answer?

TERRI: What happened to Jill? Andy.

ANDY: She came tumbling after Jack.

TEACHER : The next strategy I am going to model is clarify. Today I am only going to show you how to clarify a word. Later we will learn to clarify in other ways. The word is *f-e-t-c-h*. When I came to the word, I didn't know what it was. First I looked for chunks I knew. I knew *fet* and I knew *ch* was like the sound in chicken. I put them together and said "*fetch*." I reread the sentence and decided it must mean to get some water. Who can model how they would clarify a word? It is okay to demonstrate using a word you already know.

LARRY: I looked at the word *c-r-o-w-n*. I didn't know what it was. I knew *cr* made a sound like in the word cry. I knew -*own* made the sound like in *down*. I put *cr – own* together and said *crown*. I reread the sentence and it made sense.

TEACHER : Our last strategy is predict. What do we do when we predict?

LYNNE : We guess what is going to happen next or what we will learn.

TEACHER : What kind of guess?

LYNNE: An educated guess.

TEACHER : When I predict I use what I know and what I read to tell what might happen next. My prediction is that Jack and Jill will have to go to the doctor or hospital. Michael, what would you predict?

MICHAEL: I predict that they are going to call their HMO.

As students read more text using the reciprocal teaching process, their use of strategies will improve and, as a result, so will their comprehension.

3. After introducing students to the four strategies, have them silently read a piece of text each day under your direction. The amount of text depends on the reading ability of the students. As a rule of thumb, the

more difficulty the students are having, the shorter the text should be. Divide longer selections into several short chunks or segments of a page or just a few paragraphs. For example, if you have students read a 15- to 20-page selection, you might have them read three to four pages per day over four or five days. Each day's chunk would be further divided into chunks of several paragraphs at a time for each reciprocal teaching session. Students would silently read the designated chunk of text.

4. After reading a chunk of text, have students check any predictions they have made or answer any questions they have posed. Then model the strategy of summarize. After you model summarizing, have one or two students model the strategy. Continue the process by modeling all four strategies after reading each chunk of text. Each student does not have to model all four strategies but all four strategies should be modeled by individuals in the group. As students become better at using each strategy, they can do the initial modeling after reading a chunk. If they need more support in modeling a strategy, provide it. Gradually have the students take on more responsibility for modeling the strategies. This is scaffolding instruction.

You should notice that students' reading comprehension begins to improve in two or three weeks. For some struggling readers it may take longer before you see dramatic improvements in their reading.

Conclusion

Helping struggling readers overcome difficulties with comprehension is not a simple task, since they often have multiple difficulties. Struggling readers need systematic, continued support. For this to happen, we must assess and diagnose each student's strengths and needs—and use our findings to provide interventions that teach students how to activate their prior knowledge independently and how to use various strategies for constructing meaning or comprehending text. Although there are only a few strategies, they must be thoroughly taught. The real crux of helping struggling readers is providing many successful text reading experiences so that students can apply what they have learned. This type of systematic approach will help struggling readers overcome their comprehension difficulties.

CHAPTER 8

Writing for Struggling Readers

CASE STUDY

The seventh-grade students in Larry Michaels's language arts class are working on expository writing. They have chosen their topics; researched books, periodicals, and online resources for information related to their topics; and written first drafts. Today Larry is modeling the revision process for a group of struggling readers. He displays the following paragraph on an overhead projector:

> The electoral college should be thrown out. Everyones vote should count the same. The way we do it now, isn't right. The electoral college was made up by the guys who wrote the constitution. They don't think ordinary people were smart enough to make decisions.

Larry reads the sample paragraph aloud and asks students to think about what the author is trying to say and whether it is clear.

MR. MICHAELS: What do you think? Ready to revise? What first?

DWAYNE:	I think that second word in the first sentence is spelled wrong—or else the one later is wrong. One has gotta be wrong.
SUSAN:	Yeah—and there's places where there should be an apostrophe.
JOSE:	I think it switches—you know—from right now to something already over and back to now.
MR. MICHAELS:	Okay—good points. We will need to fix mistakes in spelling, punctuation, and grammar when we edit. But first, we are going to work on making sure the author is getting his point across. What does this author want to say?
SUSAN:	He wants the reader to agree that the—whatever—college is not the way we should vote.
JOSE:	He wants everyone's vote to count.
MR. MICHAELS:	Does he persuade you that our voting system should be changed?
INEZ:	Not me! I think there should be more details about how the electoral college works.
MR. MICHAELS:	Any other thoughts?
JOSE:	I bet some people think we shouldn't change anything. There's probably reasons why it should stay the same. Do you think the author should talk about that?
MR. MICHAELS:	Good question! Anyone have any ideas about that?
INEZ:	Yeah. If you try to talk me into something, I want to know both sides—tell me why I should and why I shouldn't—and let me make up my own mind.
MR. MICHAELS:	So, are you saying that's what this writer should do? Present both sides of the issues?

DWAYNE: No! This guy is just trying to get people to agree with him. He doesn't have to tell about that other stuff. Just leave it out. Nobody will know.

JOSE: But that isn't fair!

MR. MICHAELS: Whew! Good discussion! Here's something that might help: What is the author trying to do? Think about that and then think about how the paragraph should be revised to help the author accomplish what he was trying to do.

This is a good example of a teacher helping struggling readers think like writers. Larry's students responded to their reading by writing about what they learned. Then Larry helped them analyze a piece of writing, which will help them revise their own writing. And every time they analyze and revise their own writing, it helps them become better readers.

Why Cover Writing in a Book About Struggling Readers?

Writing and reading develop together (Tierney & Shanahan, 1991). So, more than likely, your students who struggle with reading also struggle with writing. The two processes also share many similarities:

- They contribute to the improvement of one another.

- They are ways of communicating.

- They require the same kinds of thinking, such as "What is the main idea? What do I want to say? What's the main character's problem?"

- They are necessary skills in the world outside the classroom.

- They are concerned with meaning. The purpose of writing is to convey meaning. The purpose of reading is to construct meaning.

You can help struggling students in reading and writing by helping them think like writers when they read and like readers when they write. Reading lessons should cover how writers say what they want to say. Writing lessons should cover how readers understand what the writer is trying to say. Further, struggling readers should be given chances to write in response to what they read as well as on self-selected topics.

There is also a strong connection between phonics and spelling (Adams, 1990). In a first draft, students should spell words as well as they can but keep their attention on getting their thoughts on paper or on the computer screen. But when they've finished their first draft, and have clarified their thoughts through revision, students should try to figure out the probable spelling of any words they feel they've misspelled. This will not only build their skills in spelling, but also increase their knowledge of letter-sound relationships. (See Chapter 3 for information on phonemic awareness and Chapter 4 for information on word recognition. Both topics are related to the connection between sounds and letters.) Of course, also teach students to confirm spelling using both a spell-check program on a computer and a dictionary.

Preschoolers have no hesitation about writing. The urge is there. If they have paper and pencil, or a chalkboard, or an old typewriter they will make marks, draw letters, hit keys—and call it writing. Look at a child's scribbles and ask what it is and the child will tell you "what it says." However, after starting school, some children lose that confidence and joy because, too often, their teachers tell them they didn't spell words correctly, didn't put a comma in the right place, or didn't slant a letter or cross a *t* or dot an *i* properly. If these children are struggling readers, they are apt to shrug and assume they can't write either when they get responses like those from their teachers.

If we want struggling readers to persist in their attempts to write, we must go beyond helping them decode words and comprehend when they read fiction and nonfiction. We need to help them pay attention to how those texts are structured. Understanding the structure of fiction and nonfiction not only helps students read with better comprehension, it also helps them write in those forms. Likewise, writing in those forms helps them become better readers of those forms. No matter what kind of work students do as adults, they are going to need to read and write all kinds of texts.

In this chapter we discuss two aspects of writing that struggling readers need to be taught: content and conventions. Then we explain how to apply the intervention framework to writing instruction. Finally, we give you examples of two writing lessons organized around the framework: one on revising and one on dealing with run-on sentences.

Resources for Teaching Writing

This chapter can touch only briefly on methods of teaching the content of writing. Many books have been published that will give you detailed help. Here are a few:

- *A Fresh Approach to Teaching Punctuation: Helping Young Writers Use Conventions with Precision and Purpose* by Janet Angelillo. Scholastic.

- *Making Revision Matter: Strategies for Guiding Students to Focus, Organize, and Strengthen Their Writing Independently* by Janet Angelillo. Scholastic.

- *Big Lessons From Small Writers* by Lucy M. Calkins. Heinemann.

- *Living Between the Lines* by Lucy M. Calkins. Heinemann.

- *A Fresh Look at Writing* by Donald H. Graves. Heinemann.

- *Nonfiction Writing: From the Inside Out* by Laura Robb. Scholastic.

- *Teaching Writing: Balancing Process and Product* by Gail E. Tompkins. Merrill.

- *Supporting Struggling Readers and Writers* by Dorothy S. Strickland, Kathy Ganske, and Joanne K. Monroe. Stenhouse.

Content and Conventions: Two Aspects of Writing That Need to Be Taught

Though you may have some students who write with ease and pleasure, chances are your struggling readers are not among them. We need to help struggling readers become comfortable with written language, just as we help them become comfortable with oral language. We need to help them see the connection between reading and writing, and teach strong, well-designed lessons that move them toward success in writing. To do that, we must talk about content (i.e., what kids write about) and conventions (i.e., what kids must address to make their writing presentable: spelling, grammar and usage, punctuation, and handwriting). Both areas are important.

Content

Content refers to the ideas expressed in writing—writing in any form: a written response to reading, lists, letters, journals, essays, stories, reports. Struggling readers may feel that they can't write and, therefore, often don't want to write. Writing is a chore—something that they almost always fail at. So a major part of our job is to help them see a purpose for expressing their ideas in writing, then teach them how to write, and support their increasing ability by making them feel successful.

The process of writing can be daunting even for people who enjoy writing. For struggling readers and writers, it is almost numbing. So, to help them overcome their fear, apply the intervention framework to each step of the *writing process*:

- choosing a topic and gathering information on that topic

- drafting

- revising

- editing

- publishing

You will likely need to model each step many times and guide student modeling of the step repeatedly before students can carry it out independently. Some writing does not require going through the steps outlined above for the writing process. Examples are response to reading, journals, or lists; you will need to model and guide before expecting students to write these on their own. Struggling readers are apt to feel overwhelmed even by something as natural as writing in a journal. Keeping a journal yourself and sharing it with students periodically may help.

The writing lessons for struggling readers differ from lessons for non-struggling readers mostly in terms of pacing, repetition, and the deliberate attention you give to the connection between reading and writing. (See page 174 for more information on this.) During process writing lessons, show struggling readers how their efforts bring about improvement in reading and writing. For example, as they write in a particular genre, help them recall things they have read in the same genre. As they read, talk about related writing projects they are doing.

Make writing a part of every day's activities. For example, suggest that students write in journals first thing in the morning. Collaboratively compose a group message about the day's activities. Encourage students to write notes about home-work assignments. Suggest letters to families or community leaders about a local issue. Struggling readers will soon begin to see that writing is a tool they can use.

What students want to say in writing is important. Make sure your students know that you value their thinking as much as or even more than their ability to spell or use punctuation and grammar correctly.

Conventions

Writing *conventions* refer to spelling, grammar and usage, punctuation, and legibility. Struggling readers may demonstrate problems in all of these areas and need specific, systematic instruction to overcome those problems. Keep in mind, though, that the overall purpose of writing is to convey meaning; your instruction should reinforce strongly that the reason for getting the conventions right is so that others can read and understand the writing. Here are some facts to keep in mind as you teach.

Spelling problems often accompany decoding problems. As far as we know, nobody has yet figured out a way to make everyone a good speller. Spelling well defies simple solutions. Some excellent readers are abysmal spellers, no matter how hard they work to overcome their difficulties. However, we believe that we can help most struggling readers to spell better. One important way you can help is by reinforcing the connection between phonics and spelling. The same knowledge that helps students decode words also often helps them approximate correct spelling.

Students should be taught the sound/symbol connection in both directions. That is, when you teach students to recognize a symbol and associate its sound (decoding, or reading), also be sure to teach the sound and associate its symbol (encoding, or spelling). Be aware, though, that because the English language includes many words whose spelling does not exactly match the sounds, this kind of teaching won't take care of all spelling needs.

It may also be worthwhile to help struggling students see the semantic connections between words. For example, the words *sign* and *signal* are related in meaning and, therefore, both need the letters in *sign*, even though the "*g*" is not sounded in *sign*.

Spelling some words depends on developing a spelling conscience based on visual memory (Gentry, 2004)—a sense of when a word just doesn't look right. Even if the struggling writer cannot correct the spelling, he or she can rely on spelling conscience to lead him or her to the correct spelling by consulting an electronic device, a dictionary, a friend, or a teacher.

Teach students how to use a spell-check program on the computer—and how *not* to use it. For example, the program will not catch homonyms. (The computer doesn't know whether you should have used *their* or *there*.) Also, teach students how to use a dictionary to check spelling, which means teaching them how to approximate a word's spelling closely enough to pinpoint that word in the dictionary.

Most important, help your struggling spellers overcome negative feelings about themselves as learners by teaching them how to recognize when a word may not be spelled correctly and take steps to fix it.

Grammar and usage in writing are closely related to oral language. Struggling readers will probably not use written language that is more sophisticated than their oral language when they're young. For example, the student whose oral language does not include noun-verb agreement will probably not have such agreement in his written language either. If that student uses "it don't" in oral language, you probably will see it in his written language as well. But as students get older, things should change. They should begin to express themselves in writing using more advanced language than they use in speech.

We sometimes tell children that writing is just talk written down, but that isn't always helpful. We must teach students to edit their writing for correctness even if their oral language is still not consistently correct. Eventually, they will learn that nonstandard language may sometimes be used in writing, for example, to capture the voice of a character. However, at least initially, we recommend that intervention instruction remain focused on standard usage.

Students who are given time to write learn to enjoy writing.

Punctuation and capitalization are directly connected to reading. Periods, commas, colons, and capital letters help the reader in two major ways: they help her read the text fluently, and they help her comprehend what a writer is saying. Without these signals, she wouldn't know where one thought ends and another begins. In oral language, speakers gesture, make faces, pause, drop their voices, raise their voices, or hesitate to clarify or enhance the meaning of their message. They do not run all their words together without stopping. Punctuation clarifies and enhances written messages by providing, in essence, oral language markers—familiar stopping and starting points that we recognize from speaking. As you read with struggling readers, help them notice how punctuation contributes to meaning. As you write with them, help them connect what they notice in reading to what they are composing.

Your students probably use instant messaging and e-mail, which generally requires little or no punctuation or capitalization. Be sure to let students know that these are particular kinds of recreational writing. Make clear that for school writing and for most writing in other parts of their lives, they will be expected to use punctuation and capitalization—so they need to learn to use them correctly.

Legibility is undeniably important in writing. People must be able to read what we write. They must be able to figure out if that mark on the page is an *a* or an *o*, *u*, or *n*. Most children acquire legible handwriting in the course of the usual classroom writing instruction and activities. The more they write, the more their handwriting improves.

However, since struggling readers often struggle with everything about writing, they probably also struggle with handwriting. Here are a few ideas to help you think about legibility and struggling readers.

- Legible handwriting is important. Pretty handwriting isn't.
- You can't focus on ideas and letter formation at the same time, so teach them separately.
- In the real world, you don't need cursive writing—not even to sign a check.
- Poor handwriting does not necessarily signal lack of intelligence or lack of effort.
- Learning to use a keyboard is just as useful as learning handwriting.

- "Best" handwriting should only be required when preparing a final draft for others to read—when you're finished paying attention to content or other conventions.

Applying the Intervention Framework to Writing

Recall the five steps of the intervention framework: (1) assess and diagnose, (2) teach/reteach, (3) practice, (4) apply, and (5) reassess. In this section, we apply these steps to teaching writing in general. From there, we apply them to two sample lessons related to content and conventions. You may think that these lessons are no different from any good lessons, and you would be right to a degree. However, since these lessons are designed for struggling readers, they differ from ones designed for non-struggling readers in the following ways:

- **intent:** The lesson is designed to meet particular needs.
- **focus:** The teacher keeps students' attention on a particular skill.
- **pace:** The lesson must be carried out as slowly as necessary for students to grasp the point, but quickly enough for them to catch up with their classmates.
- **repetition:** Struggling readers may need more explanation, more modeling, more practice, and more focused application than other readers.

Assess and Diagnose

Before assessing writing samples of your struggling readers, learn what they think good writing is and how they perceive themselves as writers. This can be done informally by asking open-ended questions such as these and encouraging detailed answers:

- What do you think makes a good writer? Anything else?
- What is poor writing? Is that all?
- What kind of writer are you? Why do you think so?
- What would help you be a better writer?
- Do you believe that you can improve? Why or why not?
- Explain a time when you improved your writing. How did it happen?

From there, assess your struggling readers' writing and diagnose their needs by collecting two kinds of samples early in the school year: one based on something you assign; the other based on something the student has chosen to write. Remember, you need to assess and diagnose two different broad areas of writing: content and conventions. The quickest way to gather and organize general information in both areas is to use checklists on which you can make notes. Figure 8.1 is a sample checklist for assessing writing content. Figure 8.2 is a sample checklist for assessing writing conventions. Figures 8.3 and 8.4 show these forms with teacher notes about two pieces of a student's writing.

You may assess and diagnose several aspects of writing from a single sample— for example, if a student writes a story about a lost dog at an amusement park, you might find that he has crafted a solid plot and made virtually no misspellings, but his characterization is weak, as are his grammar skills. From there, you could create an instructional plan that contains several intervention lessons based on needs, with each lesson focusing on just one area. Struggling readers and writers learn best if you keep their attention on one area and teach it thoroughly.

Even though your struggling readers may not all need help in the same areas, we suggest you teach the whole group. For those students who don't need help, the lesson will be a good refresher. After each lesson, "revisit" previously taught skills, continually reminding students to think about how what they have learned in one lesson fits into the big picture of creating meaningful writing.

Checklist for Assessing Writing Content and Process

Name _____ Grade _____ Date _____

Expository Writing

Topic _____

Organization _____

Supporting Ideas _____

Conclusions _____

_____

_____

Narrative Writing

Plot _____

Characterization _____

Problem/Resolution _____

All types of writing

Voice _____

Revision _____

Instructional Plan

_____

_____

_____

FIGURE 8.1 Checklist for assessing writing content and process

Checklist for Assessing Writing Conventions

Name _____ Grade _____ Date _____

Title and date of piece of writing evaluated _____

Spelling

Used spell-check _____

Used dictionary _____

Words misspelled _____

To work on _____

_____

Grammar/Usage

Noun-verb agreement _____

Sentence fragments _____

Run-on sentences _____

Word choice _____

To work on _____

_____

Punctuation

End punctuation _____

Capitals _____

Commas _____

To work on _____

_____

FIGURE 8.2 Checklist for assessing writing conventions: spelling, grammar/usage, punctuation

The Struggling Reader: Interventions That Work

Here are two samples of student writing that a teacher used for assessment. Figures 8.3 and 8.4 show the teacher's notes.

Joe   Sep. 10

THE CIVIL WAR
The most importent war in
are historie is the civle war.
Lincohn startrd it. He didnt lik
slavrs I dont ether. So he s
them free. And one the w
That is why I think the C
war was most importent
                    The End

Sample of expository writing
by a fourth grader

Joe   9-11

Somptimes me and my frends
play in the wods. By the river.
This one time a space ship landed
and aliyns got out and they culd
talk english and they askd us
gaestions and then they got back
into there ship and went stu
away. And we went home and
nobody belive pepple thought
we lied.

Sample of narrative writing
by a fourth grader

Checklist for Assessing Writing Conventions

Name _Joe_   Date _9-15_

Title and date of piece of writing evaluated _Civil War and_

Spelling

Used spell-check _N/A_

Used dictionary _Not observed_

Words misspelled _important, history, either,_
woods, flew

To work on: _homonyms, spelling consi_

Grammar/Usage

Noun-verb agreement _OK_   / _see "me and_
Joe's acl

Sentence fragments _several_

Run-on sentences _several_

Word choice _weak,_

To work on: _Complete sentences – mode_
"me and my friends" – model

Punctuation

End punctuation _Period missing – probabl_

Capitals _English –_

Commas _None used_

To work on: _Combine punctuation_
fragments and run-on se
→ _Review formation of_
letters – Joe uses a mi

FIGURE 8.3 Checklist for writing conventions: spelling, grammar/usage, punctuation

Checklist for Assessing Writing Content and Process

Name _Joe_   Class (grade) _4_   Date _9-15_

Expository Writing

Topic _Civil War – importance_

Organization _Poor – needs a plan and facts_

Supporting Ideas _Only gave one._

Conclusions _Not really a conclusion – just a_
restatement.

Narrative Writing   (meeting space ship)

Plot _Idea okay, but no real plot –_

Characterization _No character development._

Problem/Resolution _No problem or resolution_

All types of writing

Voice _Weak,_

Revision _No evidence of revision_

Instructional Plan

Expository – planning sheets, research, text
structure.
Narrative – analyze "story elements"

FIGURE 8.4 Checklist for assessing writing content and process

Teach/Reteach

For struggling writers, the connection between reading and writing needs to be constantly reinforced. Therefore, writing lessons for struggling readers should include reading different types of texts (narrative, compare/contrast, persuasive, and so on). Helping students recognize the structures of those different text types has been shown to help students as they plan and carry out their own writing (Gersten & Baker, 2001).

The topic of your lessons should be based on diagnosed needs, such as mastering a particular part of the writing process. You might begin by displaying an exemplary piece of writing for students to read. From there, tell students the skill they will focus on—for example, how to select a topic. Help students analyze the piece of writing for the author's use of the skill. Then model the skill yourself, using an overhead projector or computer when appropriate (Angelillo, 2005). The two sample lessons later in this chapter illustrate this kind of lesson.

Another approach is to begin with a writing task and teach students how to prepare for the task by reading. For example, if you plan a lesson on how to choose a topic, you might begin by leading students to brainstorm topics, select one that is appropriate, and then plan the kind of reading they need to do to gather information before beginning to write. Be prepared to show students how to locate information, how to determine which information is relevant and which is not, how to use search engines, how to synthesize information from several sources, how to credit sources, and so forth.

Students will most likely need help structuring their writing, so teach them the structure of text through reading and give them planning sheets that outline all of the elements they need to consider to write in that structure. Planning sheets have been shown to help students write more complete papers (Gersten & Baker, 2001). For example, if students have been studying persuasive writing, a planning sheet would help them determine their purpose, a possible lead anecdote, their main idea, evidence to support their position, and how they intend to wrap up the piece. Planning sheets can be tailored to be general or detailed, depending on students' skill level. Figures 8.5, 8.6, and 8.7 are three examples.

Planning Sheet for Persuasive Writing

Topic: _____

_____

Purpose: _____

_____

Research: _____

_____

Punch line: _____

_____

FIGURE 8.5 Planning sheet for persuasive writing, version 1

Planning Sheet for Persuasive Writing

Topic _____

Purpose _____

Ideas I want to get across:

    1. _____

    2. _____

    3. _____

People to interview to support my ideas:

    1. _____

    2. _____

    3. _____

Possible objections and how I will overcome them:

    1. _____

    2. _____

    3. _____

Summary of purpose and major points: _____

_____

Final strong statement: _____

_____

_____

FIGURE 8.6 Planning sheet for persuasive writing, version 2

The Struggling Reader: Interventions That Work

Planning Sheet for Persuasive Writing

Topic _____

Purpose _____

Research _____

    Key words to search print and Internet:

    People I can interview:

Main ideas and support for each point

    1. _____

    Interview:

    Published source:

    Internet:

    2. _____

    Interview:

    Published source:

    Internet:

    3. _____

    Interview:

    Published source:

    Internet:

Where reader can learn more (Name publications and Web sites.)

Conclusion (Restate purpose and main ideas and final strong statement.)

FIGURE 8.7 Planning sheet for persuasive writing, version 3

Practice

Struggling readers need many opportunities to practice what they have been taught. Practice activities should focus on building a particular skill, such as using end punctuation correctly, but within the context of the student's own purposeful writing. Writing should always be about something that matters to the student, in other words. Students shouldn't be told to write something simply for the sake of practicing end punctuation. However, when they edit their work, they should use what they have learned about punctuation.

Struggling readers may have particular difficulty concentrating on several tasks at once. Editing, for example, can be overwhelming for them because they're looking at spelling, punctuation, grammar, and other matters of convention simultaneously. So, we suggest teaching students to make several passes at a piece of writing during editing, looking at one area each time. They might read first for capitals and end punctuation, then read again for noun-verb agreement, then again for spelling, and so forth. If they notice other things, they can put a check mark or sticky note in the margin as a reminder to go back and check it later.

Apply

Students should apply what they are learning every time they write. When you read what students write on a daily basis, you may not need further assessment. You can also observe students informally as they write. Body language is a great diagnostic tool. Students who are struggling will have many questions, sit in front of blank paper and stare into the distance, have trouble sitting still, or crumple every effort. This signals a need for reteaching and encouragement.

Reassess

If daily writing isn't sufficient for you to determine how well a student has learned, assign a piece of writing on a particular topic for assessment purposes. Short assignments are best at first because students are more likely to experience success. At the same time, teach your struggling readers to do a self-assessment during the writing process. As they improve in their ability to evaluate their own writing, the writing itself is likely to improve. Figure 8.8 is a sample self-assessment checklist for upper-elementary or middle school struggling writers. Figure 8.9 is a sample checklist for primary-grade writers. If you make up your own checklists, ask students to help you. That way, they learn firsthand what is important to learn.

Writing Self-Evaluation Checklist

Name _____ Date _____

Before I Write My First Draft

Topic (Too big? Too narrow?) _____

Who Is Going to Read This? _____

Sources of Information

    Internet _____

    Books _____

    People to interview _____

Notes on the Main Point I Want to Make

_____

_____

_____

Notes About Supporting Ideas

_____

_____

_____

What Will I Do Next?

_____

_____

_____

FIGURE 8.8: Sample self-evaluation checklist for upper-elementary and middle school students

Am I Ready to Begin Writing?

Name _____ Date _____

What is my paper about? _____

_____

What is the most important thing I want to say?

_____

_____

_____

What else do I want to say? _____

_____

_____

_____

Where will I learn about my topic?

_____

_____

_____

What will I do next? _____

_____

_____

FIGURE 8.9: Sample self-evaluation checklist for primary-grade students

Sample Lessons Using the Intervention Framework: Revising Writing and Dealing With Run-On Sentences

Here we provide examples of two writing lessons organized around the framework: one on revising and one on dealing with run-on sentences.

A Content Lesson for Fifth-Grade Struggling Readers: Revising Writing

Assess and Diagnose Revising involves thinking: What do I want to say? To whom? Have I done what I wanted to do? Could I make my writing better? How? To assess students' ability to revise, assign them to create a piece of writing on any topic, date it, and save the first, second, and final drafts. Collect all drafts and analyze them, asking questions such as:

- Is there evidence of improvement from first draft to final copy?
- If the final draft still has problems, what are they?
- Do ideas flow logically?
- Is there irrelevant material in the first draft that is still in the final draft?
- Is there improvement in transitions from one idea to the next?
- Were words changed to be stronger or more precise?

Your instructional plan should address problems you reveal in your analysis, especially those that recur in many students' work. For example, if you find that ideas do not flow logically, transitions between paragraphs are too abrupt, and verbs are weak, plan individual lessons to address these areas. For the purposes of this sample lesson, assume that the work you analyzed revealed that students had difficulty identifying and deleting irrelevant details from their writing.

Teach/Reteach

1. Create and display a paragraph that needs revising because it contains irrelevant details, such as:

   > Voting is important. My father says everyone should vote. He doesn't like to tell anyone how he voted. He won't tell how much money he makes either. My mother doesn't care who knows. He says if you don't vote you shouldn't complain. I think voting is important.

Struggling readers benefit most from carefully modeled writing instruction.

2. Model how to improve the paragraph by thinking aloud. For example:

"In the first sentence, I need to say why I think voting is important. I'm not sure the fact that my father says everyone should vote should be here. If I leave it, I should say what his opinion has to do with what I am saying. I need to think about who will read this—that will help me decide what to include.

"In the fourth sentence, I switch from talking about the importance of voting to whether or not people should tell how they vote. I should probably take that out—my point isn't about being secretive about voting—it's about the importance of voting.

"And I certainly don't need that sentence about not telling how much money my father makes. That has nothing to do with voting.

"With all these cuts, the point is now clear, but it isn't strong enough. I say that if you don't vote you shouldn't complain—that's getting at the idea that voting is how an individual person can take part in how things are done. I need to improve that. The last sentence comes back to the first. That's good—but the sentence is weak. I need to make it stronger."

3. Go back through the text, making notes on what you plan to do as you revise. Then rewrite the piece according to those notes and display the new version. Talk with students about how the new draft is better and why.

4. Repeat this process with other paragraphs. When students seem to understand what you are doing and why, allow them to model the process using their own writing. Post a set of guidelines for students to use as they practice revising. Keep the number of guidelines small initially so that students are not overwhelmed. See Figure 8.10 for a sample.

Practice Have students select one of their own drafts to revise with an editor's eye. Encourage self-evaluation by having them ask themselves what needs to be done and why, and, once they revise, ask themselves: Did I improve this piece? In what way? Verbalizing what they do and why builds the thinking skills students need for revision.

If you have students work in partners, be sure to show them how to offer constructive criticism to improve the work rather than focus on finding weaknesses or looking for mistakes.

Apply You will know students are applying the skill when they are revising successfully without being told to. At first, you may have to remind students to use what they are learning, but soon they'll be doing it without being reminded.

Questions to Ask Myself as I Revise a Piece of Expository Writing

1. Who will read this?

2. Is my main purpose clear at the beginning?

3. Do I come back to the main purpose at the end?

4. Does every sentence relate to the purpose?

5. Should I take anything out?

6. Do I need to add anything?

7. Are the sentences in the best order?

FIGURE 8.10 A checklist for revising an expository piece

Reassess To reassess students' ability to revise, examine drafts that students have collected in their writing folders. Ask yourself the same kinds of questions you asked in your initial assessment. From there, decide whether you need to reteach the skill or can move on to a new skill.

To please their teacher, some students create multiple drafts without making substantive changes, to give the illusion of revision. If your reassessment indicates this to be the case, review the drafts with the student and help him understand that the point isn't producing drafts, it's improving the work.

Learning to revise is a lifelong process that nobody ever masters. However, with each lesson, your struggling readers should move a step closer to understanding that clear writing makes text more comprehensible. They will also move closer to being able to say exactly what they mean when they write.

A Conventions Lesson for Sixth-Grade Struggling Readers: Dealing With Run-On Sentences

Assess and Diagnose Start by examining samples of writing that students have edited, using a checklist that focuses on punctuation, such as the one in Figure 8.11. Though you may discover several punctuation problems in the samples, for purposes of this sample lesson, assume that students have a problem placing capitals at the beginning of sentences and punctuation at the end of sentences. So you plan to teach a lesson on the purpose of capital letters and periods, and how to determine when and where they are needed.

Teach

1. Display a passage with correct end punctuation, such as the one below, and read it aloud.

> When scientists work on developing a new medicine, they have to test it before the government will let them sell it for people to use. They usually test it first on animals. Some people think it is wrong to use animals this way. They think we should care as much about animals as we do humans.

Use a Think Aloud such as this to help students focus on periods. For example:

> "As I read this paragraph aloud, I know where to stop because each sentence ends with a period—and the next sentence begins with a capital. It is very clear to me as a reader. Listen as I read each sen-

Punctuation Checklist

Name _____ Date _____

Title and date of piece of writing _____

_____

	CORRECT	INCORRECT	NOTES
Periods			
Sentence fragments			
Run-on sentences			
Exclamation marks			
Questions marks			
Commas			
Colons and/or semicolons			
Dashes			
Other			

Instructional plan

_____

_____

_____

_____

FIGURE 8.11 A checklist for assessing correct use of punctuation

tence separately. Each one is a complete thought—you are not left thinking something is missing. [*Read each sentence aloud, stopping between each one to discuss how it expresses a complete thought.*] Periods and capital letters separate a person's thoughts on paper."

Lead a brief discussion about how speakers separate one thought from the next. Have students take turns saying two or more sentences and challenging others to identify by raising a hand where a sentence ends. Lead students to conclude that punctuation helps them read with understanding.

2. Display a passage without periods, such as:

> Yesterday was an important day we went to a big party for my grandparents' wedding anniversary they have been married for fifty years we all had a wonderful time.

Read the passage straight through without stopping. Then think aloud to illustrate how lack of end punctuation and capital letters makes written language difficult to understand. You might say something like:

> "I have a hard time following this paragraph because I don't know where one thought ends and the next one begins. I need to use periods and capitals." [*Illustrate by capitalizing and punctuating the paragraph accurately.*]

This is a good moment to discuss run-on sentences—grammatically incorrect sentences that run on and on without stopping, like the sample paragraph above.

Read aloud a paragraph from any text, without stopping between sentences. Read aloud another paragraph slowly, asking students to hold up a hand when they sense the end of a sentence. Tell students they can develop an ear for complete sentences by listening carefully for the way those sentences are written and combined into text. Encourage them to read their own writing aloud to determine how to punctuate it correctly.

3. Prepare a few more sample paragraphs without periods or capitals. First, model how to decide where to put periods and capitals in one of the paragraphs. Then guide student modeling of other paragraphs. Finally have students model the process without your guidance.

Student writing may contain sentence fragments punctuated as though they are complete sentences. For example, "Because she was so sad." If you

A student uses an editing checklist.

find fragments like these in students' writing, expand the lesson by demonstrating how to fix them and guiding students as they attempt to fix them on their own.

As students read and write with a new awareness of punctuation, they may notice places in books where sentence fragments are used. Be sure they understand that authors do that deliberately—to make a point. For now though, encourage students to write in complete sentences and punctuate them correctly. Later, once they understand how to use conventions, they can try fragments for stylistic purposes.

Practice The following two levels of practice are helpful to students:

1. Hand out paragraphs in need of capital letters and end punctuation and have students edit them. Tell students to read the paragraph aloud to themselves and "listen" for when a thought is complete. Do not make this a grammar lesson on subjects and predicates. The point is not to label sentence parts—it is to develop a sense of when a complete thought has been expressed in writing and what punctuation is needed to make that clear to a reader. Students may work with a partner or may work alone, comparing their marked-up paragraph with a partner when they're done.

Editing Checklist for Use Before Making a Final Copy

	YES	NO
Did I say what I wanted to say?	❑	❑
Did I have a conference with my teacher or a friend?	❑	❑
Have I used the correct words?	❑	❑
Have I checked punctuation?	❑	❑
Have I checked for run-on sentences?	❑	❑
Have I checked for sentence fragments?	❑	❑
Have I checked for noun-verb agreement?	❑	❑
Have I checked spelling of all words?	❑	❑

FIGURE 8.12 A sample editing checklist

The Struggling Reader: Interventions That Work

2. When students can accurately edit paragraphs you provide, have them use what they have learned in order to edit their own work. They should continue to rely on "listening" for complete thoughts. Partners can check each other's editing.

Apply Ideally, students will apply the new skill when they do real writing for their own purposes. At first, you will probably need to remind students to edit before making a final copy of work. Eventually, though, students will do this without being nudged by you. It helps to give students a checklist like the one in Figure 8.12 to keep in their writing folders or post near computers.

Reassess To assess student application of the skill, find a piece of writing that the student thinks is finished and ready for publication and evaluate the piece using the same checklist you used for the initial assessment and diagnosis. Based on the results, you may decide to reteach, provide more practice, or move on to an entirely new skill.

As you assess one particular skill, you may notice other areas that need teaching, reteaching, or further practice. In other words, while assessing for one skill need, you may be alerted to other skill needs. This is valuable information, so pay close attention and plan your instruction accordingly.

Lessons in punctuation are as much reading lessons as they are writing lessons because struggling readers often ignore punctuation when they read. They tend to get so bogged down decoding individual words that they disregard where sentences begin and end. But when we teach them how meaning is conveyed by using punctuation purposefully and precisely, students' reading and writing improve.

Conclusion

Struggling readers must learn to write as well as to read. As you help your students write clearly and correctly, you will also be helping them connect writing to reading. As students write, they need to think about the same things the authors of a text have thought about: What do I want to say? How do I want to organize what I say? What words shall I use? Have I spelled words and punctuated sentences correctly so that a reader can understand what I mean? As struggling readers become more successful, help them think about what they read in terms of the process the author used to create it.

Keeping Yourself Current

Recently Maria Sanchez, Mark Madro, and Betty Meyers of the Wilson School met to discuss some of the struggling readers they have in their classes. Maria, a second-grade teacher, and Mark, a fourth-grade teacher, are in their first year of teaching. Betty, a third-grade teacher, has been teaching for ten years. Here's an excerpt from their conversation:

BETTY: Has David's reading improved at all this year?

MARIA: Actually it has. He has gotten to the point that he can read and summarize at least two or three paragraphs of a second-grade-level text.

MARK: How did you get him to do that so quickly?

MARIA: I tried a technique using a graphic organizer for a story—you know, a story map. I modeled for him and then had him try it, which really seemed to help.

BETTY :   I'm not even sure what you mean by modeling for him. Where did you get that idea?

MARIA :   I heard about it from a speaker, Dr. Sparks, at a meeting I attended.

MARK :   You are always finding new ideas. How do you have time to do that and get everything else done?

BETTY :   Yeah, I can hardly stay on top of my lesson plans. Not to mention my family obligations.

MARK: Me too.

MARIA: I had a professor in college who preached about how important it was to stay current and always be looking for new ideas that work. He said it would help us to be better teachers.

MARK :   Well, just what do you do? How do you stay current?

BETTY: I would sure like to know that too.

MARIA :   Dr. Sparks talked about six steps to keep yourself current. He had a little handout that gives you tips.

MARK :   I'd like to see that.

BETTY :   Me too. Six steps, huh? That sounds doable.

MARIA :   I'll bring it to our next meeting, along with some books that Dr. Sparks told us we should have.

Clearly, remaining current about best practices for teaching reading is a priority for Maria, Mark, and Betty, as it should be for all of us. We all should know the most recent, most effective techniques to help our students succeed. It's not an easy task, given all the things on most teachers' to-do lists—writing lesson plans, preparing bulletin boards, attending meetings, completing report cards, and, of course, teaching—to mention just a few. So it is easy to put off professional reading, forgo a workshop, and avoid professional discussions with fellow teachers. But by making a commitment to do something about keeping yourself current in these ways, you are more likely to stay abreast of the best and most current ideas for helping struggling readers. In this chapter, we show you six ways to achieve that goal:

1. Join professional organizations
2. Read journals and periodicals
3. Read professional books
4. Attend workshops and classes
5. Search the Internet
6. Collaborate with colleagues

The ideas in this chapter will help you get organized and create a plan of action. Although we present these ideas separately, you should be thinking about ways to overlap them as you read. For example, you may want to organize a discussion group (idea #6) around a particularly useful article you read in

Teachers collaborate by sharing ideas.

The Reading Teacher (idea #2). Or you may want to attend a workshop (idea #4) given by the author of a favorite professional book (idea #3) so that you learn about her methods firsthand and ask questions. Be creative!

Join Professional Organizations

Numerous local, state, national, and even international professional organizations focus on reading and literacy in general, such as the International Reading Association. Others are concerned specifically with struggling readers, such as the Council for Exceptional Children's Division for Learning Disabilities. By joining one or more of these organizations, you are kept up to date in a number of ways. Attending their conferences puts you in contact with other professionals in the field. Reading their journals and newsletters keeps you in touch with the latest research and teaching ideas growing from that research. Additionally, you get to read about and/or see new programs and materials, and share your ideas with other teachers like yourself.

Talk with your colleagues to help you determine which organization to join. Ask them questions such as, Which organizations have been the most helpful to you? Which ones provide good information about struggling readers? Which organization provides the most and best journals and newsletters for teachers? Your final decision should be based on which organizations will be the most beneficial to you. Here are several organizations that provide good information on helping struggling readers:

International Reading Association (IRA)

800 Barksdale Road, Newark, DE 19714-8139, 1-800-336-7323, www.reading.org

IRA is an organization that focuses on all aspects of literacy, particularly on reading and on teaching struggling readers. It offers numerous books and periodicals, which we list in the next section.

National Council of Teachers of English (NCTE)

1111 W. Kenyon Road, Urbana, IL 61801-1096, 1-877-369-6283, www.ncte.org

NCTE focuses on all aspects of literacy—listening, speaking, reading, and writing—with emphasis on writing and literature.

International Dyslexia Association (IDA)

Chester Building, Suite 382, 8600 LaSalle Road, Baltimore, MD 21286-2044, 410-296-0232, www.interdys.org

IDA is the oldest professional organization in the country dedicated to serving people with dyslexia.

Council for Exceptional Children (CEC)

1110 North Glebe Road, Suite 300, Arlington, VA 22201-5704
1-888-CEC-SPED, Local: 703-620-3660, www.dldcec.org

Division for Learning Disabilities (DLD), one of 17 special-interest groups in the Council for Exceptional Children, focuses on the improvement of educational outcomes for students with learning disabilities. CEC also publishes numerous books related to struggling readers. You can get information on recent publications at www.cec.sped.org/bk.

Council for Learning Disabilities (CLD)

P. O. Box 4014, Leesburg, VA 20177, 571-258-1010, www.cldinternational.org

CLD is an international organization concerned with effective teaching and research related to students with learning disabilities. The organization is composed of professionals from a variety of disciplines.

Read Journals and Periodicals

There are many excellent periodicals for helping you stay current. Some of them focus on teaching ideas, some focus on research, and some on a combination of the two. We advise you to choose the ones that provide research-tested ideas that work for struggling readers. Ask yourself these questions whenever you're considering whether it will be worth your time to read an article:

- What is the research support for this suggestion? Be sure several studies are given to support the author's conclusion.

- Is it valid research? Does the research sound as if it could be replicated? Does the author give enough details so that you could try what is being suggested?

Most of the professional organizations publish a variety of journals, based on grade level and interest area. A choice of one of these journals often comes with your membership in the organization. Here are the ones that we feel will be most helpful in keeping you current about struggling readers.

International Reading Association

- *Lectura y vida* is a Spanish-language journal for all teaching levels. It provides ideas and information related to second-language learners.
- *The Reading Teacher* is a journal for preschool and elementary teachers. It often presents ideas and procedures that have been tested by classroom teachers.
- *Journal of Adolescent and Adult Literacy* is a journal for teachers of middle school, high school, and adult learners. It focuses on program design and teaching strategies.
- *Reading Research Quarterly* is a journal of research and, therefore, may not be as immediately useful, but it will give you a sense of topics that are at the forefront of scholars' and policymakers' minds.

National Council of Teachers of English

- *Language Arts* is a journal for elementary teachers that presents ideas and discussions on improving all aspects of teaching speaking, listening, reading, and writing.
- *School Talk* is a newsletter designed to keep classroom teachers in touch with current issues and ideas related to reading and writing instruction.
- *Voices From the Middle* is a newsletter for middle-school teachers. Each issue focuses on a different aspect of classroom instruction, such as writing, discussion groups, or book talks.

Division of Learning Disabilities

- *Learning Disabilities Research & Practice* is a journal that combines research with more practical articles about teaching students with learning disabilities.

Council for Learning Disabilities

- *Learning Disabilities Quarterly* is a research journal that focuses on the more theoretical aspects of learning disabilities. It presents new ideas to try and test in your classroom and informs you of the direction research is going.
- *Intervention in School and Clinic* is another journal that provides practical research-based ideas.

Read Professional Books

Reading professional books is another good way to keep yourself current. There are always new books coming on the market. In fact, the biggest challenge here is deciding which books to read. Throughout this book, we have referred to many good ones; you might want to go back and look for ones that suit your needs. We also suggest considering conference and workshop speakers' recommendations and ads in the journals you read. You might also periodically go to an Internet bookstore such as www.amazon.com, type "struggling readers" into the search engine, and peruse the list of titles that appear. As we were writing this text, we tried this and got more than 91,000 entries with brief descriptions, listed in order of highest sales. Some even had readers' comments. By checking Internet bookstores periodically, you will know what's new and what professionals like you are reading. You can also visit the Web sites of publishers of professional books for teachers, such as:

Christopher Gordon: www.christopher-gordon.com

Guilford Press: www.guilford.com

Heinemann: www.heinemann.com

Newbridge: www.newbridgeonline.com

Pro-Ed: www.proedinc.com

Scholastic Teaching Resources: www.scholastic.com

Stenhouse: www.stenhouse.com

If you live near a college that offers reading education classes, check out the bookstore to see what texts are being assigned to students.

Attend Workshops and Classes

Another way to keep current is by attending workshops and taking courses on a variety of topics related to reading instruction. If your school district offers courses, classes, and workshops, take advantage of them. Also, watch for ads and flyers in your school advertising courses and workshops at local colleges and universities. In addition, some private companies offer training on a variety of reading-related topics. Here are three of the better-known ones:

Bureau of Education & Research (BER)

P. O. Box 96068, Bellevue, WA 98009-9668, 1-800-735-3503, www.ber.org

Charlesbridge Seminars

85 Main Street, Watertown, MA 02472-4411, 1-800-225-3214
www.charlesbridge.com/school/html/professional.html

Staff Development Resources (SDR)

2535 West 237th Street, Suite 126, P. O. Box 3168, Torrance, CA 90505,
1-800-678-8908, www.sdresources.org

Finally, consider training that publishers offer in connection with their reading programs. We suggest that you check with sales representatives to see what is being offered in your area.

Search the Internet

The Internet is a valuable resource for information on struggling readers, so search it periodically. Type the topic "struggling readers" into your browser's search engine or go directly to www.google.com or www.yahoo.com and do the same thing. You will find hundreds of sites offering articles, lesson plans, and other resources related to struggling readers. You should always double-check information that you find against other sources, such as other Web sites, journals, and the most current professional books to be sure it is reliable.

By searching the Internet, you can also find opportunities to network with other teachers. In other words, get to know individuals who do the same type of work you do. Many schools and educational programs have their own Web pages. By tapping into those Web pages, you can find teachers with students who have problems similar to those of your students, and establish a dialogue. Here are some Web sites that will help you get started with online networking.

Pathways to Literacy

www.tiill.com

This site gives teachers resources, links to professional organizations, a live chat line, and a news forum related to aspects of literacy, including struggling readers.

Teachers search the Internet together for information
to help them teach struggling readers.

Illinois Literacy Resource Development Center

www.ilrdc.org

This site provides information on different professional development programs
in 14 different locations throughout Illinois.

Foundation for California Early Literacy Learning

www.cell-exll.com

This site helps elementary teachers strengthen their reading and writing instruction.

The Learning Space (Washington State)

www.learningspace.org

This site presents information about literacy programs, funding sources, and
classroom Web pages, and online tutorial training modules.

Collaborate With Colleagues

Collaborating with your colleagues is another valuable way to continue your professional growth. We suggest that you designate a regular time to meet with other teachers and specialists in your building or district to discuss the growth and needs of specific students, share ideas, and raise questions. Here are some other ways to promote collaboration within your school:

- Use faculty meetings to discuss instructional matters related to specific students, as well as general curriculum matters. If your faculty meetings currently don't allow for this type of discussion, ask your principal if it would be possible to change the format.

- Have grade-level or team meetings to review the progress of individual students.

- Schedule times to visit other teachers' classrooms. After the visit, meet with the teacher at a convenient time to discuss what you saw.

- Videotape a lesson with some of your struggling readers and ask other colleagues to meet and discuss it with you.

- Share new books, articles, and other resources with colleagues.

- Attend professional meetings with several other teachers. This will allow you time to discuss what you learn.

Making Your Own Plan

Take a few minutes to jot down one or two things that you haven't done before but want to do over the next few months, based on what's been discussed in this chapter. For example, Mark Madro, one of the teachers we met at the beginning of the chapter, joined the IRA and plans to look for one article each month that he can share with other teachers. Betty plans to attend a seminar on teaching struggling readers at the local college. Make your own plan. Work on it. At the end of two months, review what you have done. Make changes as needed. Every struggling reader deserves the best teacher possible—the teacher who strives to ensure that every struggling reader makes more than adequate yearly progress to be the best reader he or she can be.

Glossary

accuracy In reading, saying the correct words and heeding punctuation.

advanced word recognition The ability to decode words with unexpected letter-sound correspondence by the use of analogy or memory for word types.

affix Word part attached to the beginning or ending of a base or root word that changes its meaning. Prefixes, suffixes, and inflected endings are all affixes.

alphabetic principle The concept that speech sounds are represented by graphic symbols.

antonym Word that is opposite in meaning to another word.

apply The fourth step of the intervention framework. Learners use a skill in a real situation.

assisted reading (see *coached reading*)

authentic Not designed to be part of the instructional materials. In literacy this usually refers to tasks and materials related to actual reading and writing not related directly to instruction.

automaticity Identifying letters, sounds, or words quickly and effortlessly.

blending The ability to pronounce several sounds together to produce a word part or a word.

bound morpheme A morpheme that has meaning only when combined with another morpheme.

coached reading Reading with the help of another.

collaborating (collaboration) Working with other professionals toward a goal.

comprehension Understanding of what one has heard, seen, or read.

consonant blend Two or more consonants in a single syllable making a single sound but in which each consonant sound can be heard.

consonant digraph Two consonants together producing one sound.

content As a component of oral language, the vocabulary a person knows and uses.

content In writing, the ideas that a writer expresses in whatever form he or she is using.

continuous sound Uninterrupted flow of sound such as is possible when saying the vowels or certain consonants (such as *m* or *n*).

convention In writing, acceptable standard of spelling, grammar, and usage.

decodability A quality of a word that can be identified by applying phonics.

decodable text Text that is limited to words a student can identify using skills that have been learned or by recognizing sight words.

diagnostic assessment or tool Test or other way to determine specific problem areas as well as strengths.

diphthong Two vowels together in one syllable producing a blend of the two sounds. The *ou* in *house* is a diphthong.

drafting The step in the writing process in which one composes.

editing The step in the writing process in which one corrects errors in spelling, usage, grammar, punctuation, and sentence structure.

fluency In reading, the ability to read connected text smoothly and without word-recognition problems.

form As a component of oral language, the phonology, morphology, and syntax of a language.

free (unbound) morpheme A morpheme that has meaning by itself.

function The use, or pragmatics, of language.

identifying important information The ability to determine the main ideas in a text.

inferring/predicting Drawing conclusions or predicting future events based on background knowledge and what one has heard or read to a certain point.

informal reading inventory A measure of reading levels; sometimes yields diagnostic information.

intervention Providing instruction to struggling readers to stop further failure and help them make adequate yearly progress.

irregular word Word in which letters do not represent the expected or common sound. Such a word must be identified by means other than phonics alone.

iteration Repetition of a single sound.

key concept vocabulary Words that a reader must recognize and understand in order to read a certain text.

letter-sound correspondence The relationship between letters (graphic symbols) and the sounds the letters stand for.

letter-sound relationship (see *letter-sound correspondence*)

meaning vocabulary Words that an individual understands and can use, whether or not the word is recognized in print.

monitoring/clarifying Recognizing when one doesn't understand something and taking steps to rectify that lack of understanding.

morpheme A meaningful unit of language.

morphology The study of the structure and forms of words.

onset The part of a syllable or one-syllable word that precedes the vowel sound. In the word *tack*, *t* is the onset. In the word *stack*, *st* is the onset.

oral reading fluency (see *fluency*)

oral vocabulary Words an individual understands when heard and can use when speaking.

orthography The writing system of a language.

phoneme The smallest unit of sound in a language.

phonemic awareness The ability to hear and produce the separate sounds in a word and to blend separate sounds into words.

phonics A way of teaching word recognition that is based on the relationship between letters and the sounds the letters represent.

phonological awareness Awareness of sounds in a language: syllables, onsets and rimes, or individual phonemes (phonemic awareness).

phonology The study of speech sounds and their functions.

pitch The rise and fall of speech.

practice The third step of the intervention framework. Learners repeat a just-taught skill first with guidance and then independently.

pragmatics The practical uses of language.

prefix Word part affixed to the beginning of a base or root word that changes the meaning of that word.

prevention Identifying potential struggling readers and providing appropriate instruction so that failure is avoided.

previewing A strategy for looking at elements of a text before reading in order to activate prior knowledge and make predictions.

print vocabulary Words an individual recognizes when seen in print.

prior knowledge Background a reader has for understanding a particular text.

progress monitoring assessment or tool Test or other means to measure progress a learner is making toward a goal.

pronoun referent The noun to which a pronoun refers.

prosody The pitch, loudness, stress, rhythm, and tempo of spoken language.

publishing The final step in the writing process, in which a piece of writing is made available in some way for others to read.

questioning The ability to generate questions about text and then read to answer one's own questions.

rate Reading speed, usually reported as the average number of correct words read per minute.

r-controlled vowel Vowel whose sound is altered when followed by the letter *r*, as in words such as *star*, *her*, or *for*.

reciprocal teaching An interactive process in which teacher and students take turns modeling the use of strategies.

recognition vocabulary Words an individual recognizes and can say when seen in print.

regular word Word in which letters represent the usual or expected sounds. Such a word is decodable by applying phonics knowledge.

remediation A term previously used to describe instruction given to struggling readers, suggesting that teachers should wait until a student is already failing and then correct problems.

revising The step in the writing process that follows drafting; the writer examines the content of what he or she has written and rewrites in order to improve it.

rime The part of a syllable or one-syllable word that includes the vowels and the sounds that follow the vowel. In the word *tack*, *-ack* is the rime.

scaffolded instruction Instruction that provides whatever support students need; implies beginning with a great deal of support from a teacher, which is gradually withdrawn until students are able to perform a task independently.

screening assessment or tool Tests that measure a student's performance on a given task in order to determine the likelihood that the student is going to experience difficulties; usually refers to standardized tests, those where typical performance of students at different ages has been determined.

segment The ability to hear a word (or group of sounds) and separate and produce the individual sounds.

semantics The meanings of words (and groups of words).

shared reading A method in which the teacher reads aloud and invites students to join in whenever they feel comfortable doing so; a level of scaffolded support.

sight word Word recognized instantly without the need to analyze. Also used to refer to words that must be memorized because they do not follow spelling generalizations or words that students must learn by sight because they do not yet have the skills to decode them.

sound segment An individual sound.

stop sound A sound in the language in which breath is interrupted and the sound cannot be sustained; the letters hard *c*, *t*, and *p* are examples of stop sounds.

strategy Plan for dealing with an unfamiliar task.

stress A word that is given emphasis. Sometimes referred to as being accented.

struggling reader Any reader who is not reading fluently and with good comprehension in grade-level material.

subskill A skill that is part of a larger or more complex skill.

suffix Word part affixed to the ending of a base or root word that changes the meaning; sometimes understood to include inflectional endings.

summarizing Retelling the main ideas and supporting details of expository text or the basic story of narrative text.

synonyms Two or more words that mean the same or very nearly the same.

syntax The word order in sentences or phrases.

synthesizing Combining information from more than one source into one coherent whole.

teach The second step of the intervention framework. The teacher uses the results of assessment and diagnosis to plan and provide direct, explicit instruction by modeling, guiding student modeling, and then having students model a new skill.

tone Inflections in speech that indicate meaning.

visualizing The ability to imagine scenes or events when reading.

vocabulary Those words known by an individual; may be thought of as made up of oral language vocabulary, recognition vocabulary, and meaning vocabulary.

vowel digraph Two vowels together in one syllable making one sound. The *ea* in *read*, *oa* in *road*, and *ai* in *pail* are examples of vowel digraphs.

vowel-consonant-e pattern This pattern of letters in a word often signals that the first vowel is long, while the final *e* is not sounded. An example of such a word is *hope*.

word bank/word book Individual collection of words learned.

writing process Sometimes called "process writing," this usually refers to all parts of writing from choosing a topic through writing a draft, revising, editing, and publishing.

Professional References Cited

Adams, M. J. (1990). *Beginning to read: Thinking and learning about print*. Cambridge, MA: MIT Press.

Alexander, P. A., & Jetton, T. L. (2000). Learning from text: A multidimensional and developmental perspective. In M. L. Kamil, P. B. Mosenthal, P. D. Pearson, & R. Barr (Eds.), *Handbook of reading research*, Vol. 3 (pp. 285–310), Mahwah, NJ: Lawrence Erlbaum Associates.

Allen, J. (1999). *Words, words, words: Teaching vocabulary in grades 4–12*. Portland, ME: Stenhouse.

Allington, R. L. (2001). *What really matters for struggling readers*. New York: Longman.

Allington, R. L., & Walmsley, S. A. (Eds.). (1995). *No quick fix: Rethinking literacy programs in America's elementary schools*. New York: Teachers College Press.

The American Heritage Dictionary (3rd ed.). (1992). Boston: Houghton Mifflin Company.

Anderson, R. C., Hiebert, E. H., Scott, J. A., & Wilkinson, I. A. G. (1985). *Becoming a nation of readers: The report of the Commission on Reading*. Washington, DC: National Institute of Education.

Anderson, R. C., & Pearson, P. D. (1984). A schema-theoretic view of basic processes in reading comprehension. In P. D. Pearson (Ed.), *Handbook of reading research*, (pp. 255–291). New York: Longman.

Angelillo, J. (2005). *Making revision matter: Strategies for guiding students to focus, organize, and strengthen their writing independently*. New York: Scholastic.

Angelillo, J. (2005). *A fresh approach to teaching punctuation: Helping young writers use conventions with precision and purpose*. New York: Scholastic.

Baumann, J. F., & Kame'enui, E. J. (Eds.). (2004). *Vocabulary instruction: Research to practice*. New York: Guilford.

Beck, I. (1998). Understanding beginning reading: A journey through teaching and research. In J. Osborn & F. Lehr (Eds.), *Literacy for all* (pp. 11–31). New York: Guilford.

Beck, I., & McKeown, M. (1991). Conditions of vocabulary acquisition. In R. Barr, M. L. Kamil, P. B. Mosenthal, & P. D. Pearson (Eds.), *Handbook of reading research* (Vol. 2, pp. 789–814). New York: Longman.

Beck, I. L., & McKeown, M. G. (2001). Text talk: Capturing the benefits of read-aloud experiences for young children. *The Reading Teacher, 55*(1), 10–20.

Beck, I. L., McKeown, M. G., & Kucan, L. (2002). *Bringing words to life: Robust vocabulary instruction*. New York: Guilford Press.

Beck, I. L., McKeown, M. G., & Omanson, R. C. (1987). The effects and uses of diverse vocabulary instructional techniques. In M. G. McKeown & M. E. Curtis (Eds.), *The nature of vocabulary acquisition*. Hillsdale, NJ: Lawrence Erlbaum Associates.

Betts, E. A. (1946). *Foundations of reading instruction*. New York: American Book.

Biemiller, A. (2001). Teaching vocabulary: Early, direct, and sequential. *The American Educator, 25*(1), 24–28.

Blachowicz, C. & Fisher, P. (1996). *Teaching vocabulary in all classrooms*. Upper Saddle River, NJ: Prentice Hall.

Blachowicz, C. L. Z., & Fisher, P. (2000). Vocabulary instruction. In M. L. Kamil, P. B. Mosenthal, P. D. Pearson, & R. Barr (Eds.), *Handbook of reading research* (Vol. 3, pp. 503–523). Mahwah, NJ: Lawrence Erlbaum Associates.

Blachowicz, C. L. Z., & Fisher, P. (2004). Building vocabulary in remedial settings: Focus on word relatedness. *Perspectives, 30*(1), 24–31.

Block, C. C., & Mangieri, J. N. (Eds.) (in press). *The vocabulary-enriched classroom: Practices for improving the reading performance of all students in grades 3 and up*. New York: Scholastic.

Burns, P. C., & Roe, B. D. (2002). *Burns/Roe informal reading inventory* (Preprimer to twelfth grade) (6th ed., revised by B. D. Roe). Boston: Houghton Mifflin.

Calkins, L. M. (1990). *Living between the lines*. Portsmouth, NH: Heinemann.

Carnine, D. W., Silbert, J., Kame'enui, E. J., & Tarver, S. (2004). *Direct instruction reading* (4th ed.). Upper Saddle River, NJ: Prentice Hall.

Carver, R. P., & Hoffman, J. V. (1981). The effect of practice through repeated reading on gain in reading ability using a computer-based instructional system. *Reading Research Quarterly, 16*(3), 374–390.

Chall, J. S. (1987). Two vocabularies for reading: Recognition and meaning. In M. G. McKeown & M. E. Curtis (Eds.), *The nature of vocabulary acquisition* (pp. 7–17). Hillsdale, NJ: Lawrence Erlbaum Associates.

Chall, J. S., & Curtis, M. E. (2003). Children with reading difficulties. In J. Flood, D. Lapp, J. R. Squire, & J. M. Jensen (Eds.), *Handbook of research on teaching the English language arts* (2nd ed.). (pp. 413–420). Mahwah, NJ: Lawrence Erlbaum Associates.

Chard, D. J., & Dickson, S. V. (1999). Phonological awareness: Instructional and assessment guidelines. *Intervention in School and Clinic, 34*, 261-270.

Chard, D. J., & Osborn, J. (1999). Phonics and word recognition instruction in early reading programs: guidelines for accessibility. *Learning Disabilities Research and Practice, 14*(2), 107–117.

Chard, D. J., Simmons, D. C., & Kame'enui, E. J. (1998). Word recognition: Research bases. In D. C. Simmons & E. J. Kame'enui (Eds.), *What reading research tells us about children with diverse learning needs: Bases and basics* (pp. 141–167). Mahwah, NJ: Lawrence Erlbaum Associates.

Chard, D. J., Vaughn, S., & Tyler, B. J. (2002). A synthesis of research on effective interventions for building fluency with elementary students with learning disabilities. *Journal of Learning Disabilities, 35*, 386–406.

Committee on the Prevention of Reading Difficulties (1998). *Preventing reading difficulties in young children.* Washington, DC: National Academy Press.

Cooper, J. D. (2006). *Literacy: Helping children construct meaning* (6th ed.). Boston: Houghton Mifflin.

Cooper, J. D., Boschken, I., McWilliams, J., & Pistochini, L. (2000). A study of the effectiveness of an intervention program designed to accelerate reading for struggling readers in the upper grades. In T. Shanahan & F. V. Rodriguez-Brown (Eds.), *National reading conference yearbook 49* (pp. 477–486). Chicago: National Reading Conference.

Cooper, J. D., & Kiger, N. D. (2005). *Literacy assessment: Helping teachers plan instruction* (Second Edition). Boston: Houghton Mifflin.

Cunningham, A., & Stanovich, K. E. (1998). What reading does to the mind. *American Educator, 22,* 8–15

Cunningham, P. M., & Allington, R. L. (2003). *Classrooms that work: They can all read and write* (3rd ed.). Boston: Allyn & Bacon.

Daly, E. J., & Martens, B. K. (1994). A comparison of three interventions for increasing oral reading performance: Application of the instructional hierarchy. *Journal of Applied Behavior Analysis, 27,* 459–469.

Dowhower, S. L. (1991). Effects of repeated reading on second-grade transitional readers' fluency and comprehension. *Reading Research Quarterly, 22,* 389–406.

Ehri, L. C. (1995). Stages of development in learning to read words by sight. *Journal of Research in Reading, 18,* 116–125.

Ehri, L. C. (1998). Research on learning to read and spell: A personal-historical perspective. *Scientific Studies of Reading, 2,* 97–114.

Ehri, L. C. (1999). Phases of development in learning to read words. In J. Oakhill, & R. Beard (Eds.), *Reading development and the teaching of reading: A psychological perspective* (pp. 79–108). Malden, MA: Blackwell.

Ehri, L. C. (2005). Learning to read words: Theory, findings, and issues.

Scientific Studies of Reading, 9, 167–188.

Fey, M. E., Catts, H. W., & Larrivee, L. S. (1995). Preparing preschoolers for the academic and social challenges of school. In M. E. Fey, J. Windsor, & S. F. Warren (Eds.), *Communication and language intervention series: Vol. 5. Language intervention: preschool through elementary years* (pp. 3–37). Baltimore: Brookes.

Fielding, L. G., Wilson, P. T., & Anderson, R. C. (1986). A new focus on free reading: The role of tradebooks in reading instruction. In T. E. Raphael (Ed.), *Contexts of school-based literacy* (pp. 149–160). New York: Random House.

Fleisher, L. S., Jenkins, J. R., & Pany, D. (1979–80). Effects on poor readers' comprehension of training in rapid decoding. *Reading Research Quarterly, 15,* 30–48.

Fuchs, L. S., Fuchs, D., Hamlett, C. L., Walz, L., & Germann, G. (1993). Formative evaluation of academic progress: How much growth can we expect? *School Psychology Review, 22,* 27–48.

Gentry, J. R. (2004). *The science of spelling.* Portsmouth, NH: Heinemann.

Gentry, J. R. & Gillet, J. W. (1993). *Teaching kids to spell.* Portsmouth, NH: Heinemann.

Gersten, R., & Baker, S. (2001). Teaching expressive writing to students with learning disabilities: A meta-analysis. *The Elementary School Journal, 101,* 251–272.

Good, R. H., & Kaminski, R. A. (2002). *Dynamic indicators of basic early literacy skills* (6th ed.). Eugene, OR: Institute for the Development of Educational Achievement.

Graves, M. F. (1994). *A fresh look at writing.* Portsmouth, NH: Heinemann.

Graves, M. F. (1986). Vocabulary learning and instruction. *Review of Research in Education, 13,* 91–128.

Graves, M. F. (1987). The roles of instruction in fostering vocabulary development. In M. G. McKeown & M. E. Curtis (Eds.), *The nature of vocabulary acquisition* (pp. 165–184). New York: Lawrence Erlbaum Associates.

Harris, T. L., & Hodges, R. E. (1995). *The literacy dictionary.* Newark, DE: International Reading Association.

Hart, B., & Risley, T. R. (1995). *Meaningful differences in the everyday experiences of American children.* Baltimore: Paul Brookes.

Hasbrouck, J. E., & Tindal, G. (1992). Curriculum-based oral reading fluency norms for students in grades 2 through 5. *Teaching Exceptional Children, 24,* 41–44.

Hiebert, E. H., & Taylor, B. M. (Eds.). (1994). *Getting reading right from the start: Effective early literacy interventions.* Boston: Allyn & Bacon.

Huey, E. B. (1908). *The psychology of reading.* New York: Macmillan.

Hurley, S., & Tinajero, J. (2001). *Literacy assessment of second language learners.* Allyn & Bacon: Boston.

Johns, J. L. (2001). *Basic Reading Inventory* (preprimer through grade twelve and early literacy assessments) (8th ed.). Dubuque, IA: Kendall/Hunt.

Johnson, D. D., & Pearson, P. D. (1984). *Teaching reading vocabulary* (2nd ed.). New York: Holt, Rinehart and Winston.

Juel, C., & Roper-Schneider, D. (1985). The influence of basal readers on first-grade reading. *Reading Research Quarterly, 20,* 134–152.

Juel, C., Griffith, P. L., & Gough, P. B. (1986). Acquisition of literacy: A longitudinal study of children in first and second grade. *Journal of Educational Psychology, 78,* 243–255.

Kaminski, R. A., & Good, R. H. (1996). Toward a technology for assessing basic early literacy skills. *School Psychology Review, 25,* 215–227.

Kuhn, M. R., & Stahl, S. A. (2000). *Fluency: A review of developmental and remedial practices.* Ann Arbor, MI: Center for the Improvement of Early Reading Achievement.

LaBerge, D., & Samuels, S. J. (1974). Towards a theory of automatic information processing in reading. *Cognitive Psychology, 6,* 293–323.

Learning First Alliance (1998). *Every child reading: An action plan.* Washington, DC: Learning First Alliance.

Leslie, L. & Caldwell, J. (2001). *Qualitative Reading Inventory 3* (emergent through high school). Boston: Allyn & Bacon.

Levy, B. A., Abello, B., & Lysynchuk, L. (1997). Transfer from word training to reading in context: Gains in fluency and comprehension. *Learning Disability Quarterly, 20,* 173–188.

Liberman, I. Y., Shankweiler, D., Fischer, F. W., & Carter, B. (1974). Explicit syllable and phoneme segmentation in the young child. *Journal of Experimental Child Psychology, 18,* 201–212.

Liberman, I. Y., Shankweiler, D., & Liberman, A. M. (1989). The alphabetic principle and learning to read. In D. Shankweiler, & I. Y. Liberman (Eds.), *Phonology and reading disability: Solving the reading puzzle* (pp. 1–33). Ann Arbor: University of Michigan Press.

Loban, W. D. (1963). *The language of elementary school children.* Champaign, IL: National Council of Teachers of English.

Lorge, I. & Chall, J. S. (1963). Estimating the size of vocabularies of children and adults: An analysis of methodological issues. *Journal of Experimental Education, 32,* 147–157.

McKenna, M. C. (2004). Teaching vocabulary to struggling older readers. *Perspectives 30,* 1, 13–16.

McKeown, M. G., & Curtis, M. E. (1987). *The nature of vocabulary acquisition.* Hillsdale, NJ: Lawrence Erlbaum Associates.

Monda, L. E. (1989). *The effects of oral, silent, and listening repetitive reading on the fluency and comprehension of learning disabled students.* Doctoral dissertation, Florida State University, Tallahassee.

Morrow, L. M. (1989). Using story retelling to develop comprehension. In K. D. Muth (Ed.), *Children's comprehension of text: Research into practice* (pp. 37-58). Newark, DE: International Reading Association.

Nagy, W. E. (1988). *Teaching vocabulary to improve reading comprehension.* Newark, DE/Urbana, IL: IRA/NCTE.

Nagy, W. E., & Anderson, R. C. (1984). How many words are there in printed school English? *Reading Research Quarterly, 19,* 304–330.

Nagy, W. E., & Herman, P. A. (1987). Breadth and depth of vocabulary knowledge: Implications for acquisition and instruction. In M. G. McKeown & M. E. Curtis (Eds.), *The nature of vocabulary acquisition* (pp. 19–35). Hillsdale, NJ: Lawrence Erlbaum Associates.

Nathan, R. G., & Stanovich, K. E. (1991). The causes and consequences of differences in reading fluency. *Theory Into Practice, 30*(3), 176–184.

National Reading Panel (2000). *Teaching children to read: An evidence-based assessment of the scientific research literature on reading and its implications for reading instruction.* Washington, DC: National Academy Press.

National Research Council (1998). *Preventing reading difficulties in young children.* Washington, DC: National Academy Press.

Oczkus, L. D. (2003). *Reciprocal teaching at work: Strategies for improving reading comprehension.* Newark, DE: International Reading Association.

O'Shea, L. J., Sindelar, P. T., & O'Shea, D. J. (1987). The effects of repeated readings and attentional cures on the reading fluency and comprehension of learning disabled reading. *Learning Disabilities Research, 2,* 103–109.

Palincsar, A. S., & Brown, A. L. (1984). Reciprocal teaching of comprehension-fostering and comprehension-monitoring activities. *Cognition and Instruction, 1(2),* 117–175.

Paris, S. G., Wasik, B. A., & Turner, J. C., (1991). The development of strategic readers. In R. Barr, M. Kamil, P. B. Mosenthal, & P. D. Pearson (Eds.), *Handbook of reading research, Vol. II* (pp. 609–640). New York: Longman.

Perfetti, C. A., Beck, I., Bell, L., & Hughes, C. (1987). Phonemic knowledge and learning to read are reciprocal: A longitudinal study of first grade children. *Merrill-Palmer Quarterly, 33,* 283–319.

Pikulski, J. J. (1994). Preventing reading failure: A review of five effective programs. *The Reading Teacher, 48*(1), 30-39.

Pikulski, J. J., & Chard, D. J. (2005). Fluency: Bridge between decoding and reading comprehension. *The Reading Teacher, 58*(6), 510–519.

Pinnell, G. S., Pikulski, J. J., Wixson, K. K., Campbell, J. R., Gough, P. B., & Beatty, A. S. (1995). *Listening to children read aloud.* Washington, DC: Office of Educational Research and Improvement, U. S. Department of Education.

Rasinski, T. V. (2003). *The fluent reader.* New York: Scholastic.

Rasinski, T. V., & Hoffman, J. V. (2003). Oral reading in the school literacy curriculum. *Reading Research Quarterly, 38,* 510–522.

Rasinski, T. V., & Padak, N. (2005). *3-minute reading assessments: Word recognition, fluency & comprehension, grades 1-4.* New York: Scholastic.

Rasinski, T. V., & Padak, N. (2005). *3-minute reading assessments: Word recognition, fluency & comprehension, grades 5–8.* New York: Scholastic.

Rayner, K., & Pollatsek, A. (1989). *The psychology of reading.* Englewood Cliffs, NJ: Prentice Hall.

Robb, L. (2004). *Nonfiction writing from the inside out.* New York: Scholastic.

Rose, T. L., & Beattie, J. R. (1986). Relative effects of teacher-directed and taped previewing on oral reading. *Learning Disabilities Quarterly, 9,* 193–199.

Seashore, R. H. (1947). How many words do children know? *The Packet, 2,* 3–17.

Shaywitz, S. E. (2003). *Overcoming dyslexia: A new and complete science-based program for reading problems at any level.* New York: Knopf.

Shefelbine, J. (1996). *Basic phonics skills test.* Sacramento, CA: California State University.

Simmons, D. C., & Kame'enui, E. J. (Eds.) (1998). *What reading research tells us about children with diverse learning needs: Bases and basics*. Mahwah, NJ: Lawrence Erlbaum Associates.

Smith, S. B., Simmons, D. C., & Kame'enui, E. J. (1998). Phonological awareness: Bases. In D. C. Simmons & E. J. Kame'enui (Eds.), *What reading research tells us about children with diverse learning needs: Bases and basics* (pp. 61–128). Mahwah, NJ: Lawrence Erlbaum Associates.

Snow, C., Burns, M. S., & Griffin, P. (Eds.) (1998). *Preventing reading difficulties in young children*. Washington, DC: National Academy Press.

Stahl, S. A. (1998). *Vocabulary development*. Brookline, MA: Brookline Books.

Stahl, S. A. (2004). Vocabulary learning and the child with learning disabilities. *Perspectives, 30*(1), 5–12.

Stahl, S. A., & Fairbanks, M. M. (1986). The effects of vocabulary instruction: A model-based meta-analysis. *Review of Educational Research, 56* (1), 72–110.

Stahl, S. A., & Kapinus, B. A. (1991). Possible sentences: Predicting word meanings to teach content area vocabulary. *The Reading Teacher, 45*, 36–43.

Stanovich, K. E. (1980). Toward an interactive-compensatory model of individual differences in the development of reading fluency. *Reading Research Quarterly, 16*, 32–71.

Stanovich, K. E. (1986). Matthew effects in reading: Some consequences of individual differences in the acquisition of literacy. *Reading Research Quarterly, 21*, 360–407.

Stanovich, K. E. (1991). Word recognition: Changing perspectives. In R. Barr, M. L. Kamil, P. B. Mosenthal, and P. D. Pearson (Eds.), *Handbook of reading research* (Vol. 2, pp. 418–452). New York: Longman.

Stanovich, K. E., & Cunningham, A. E. (1992). Studying the consequences of literacy within a literate society: The cognitive correlates of print exposure. *Memory & Cognition, 20*(1), 51–68.

Strickland, D. S., Ganske, K., & Monroe, J. K. (2001) *Supporting struggling readers and writers*. Portland, ME: Stenhouse.

Taba, H. (1967). *Teacher's handbook for elementary school social studies*, Reading, MA: Addison-Wesley.

Tan, A., & Nicholson, T. (1997). Flashcards revisited: Training poor readers to read words faster improves their comprehension of text. *Journal of Educational Psychology, 89*(2), 276–288

Tierney, R. J., & Shanahan, T. (1991). Research on the reading-writing relationship: Interactions, transactions, and outcomes. In R. Barr, M. L. Kamil, P. B. Mosenthal, & P. D. Pearson (Eds.), *Handbook of Reading Research* (Vol. 2, pp. 246–280). White Plains, NY: Longman.

Tompkins, G. E. (2003). *Teaching writing: Balancing process and product*. Upper Saddle River, NJ: Merrill.

Torgesen, J. K., Wagner, R. K, & Rashotte, C. A. (1994). Longitudinal studies of phonological processing and reading. *Journal of Learning Disabilities, 27*(5) 276–286.

Troia, G. A., Roth, F. P., & Graham, S. (1998). An educator's guide to phonological awareness: Assessment measures and intervention activities for children. *Focus on Exceptional Children, 31*(3), 1–12.

U.S. Department of Education, National Center for Education Statistics. (1995). *Listening to children read aloud*. Washington, DC: Author.

Vaughn, S., Gersten, R., & Chard, D. J. (2000). The underlying message in LD intervention research: Findings from research syntheses. *Exceptional Children, 67*, 99–114.

Whipple, G. (ed.). (1925). *The Twenty-fourth Yearbook of the National Society for the Study of Education: Report of the National Committee on Reading*. Bloomington, IL: Public School Publishing Company.

White, T. G., Graves, M. F., & Slater, W. H. (1990). Growth of reading vocabulary in diverse elementary schools: Decoding and word meaning. *Journal of Educational Psychology, 82*, 281–290.

White, T. G., Sowell, J., & Yanagihara, A. (1989). Teaching elementary students to use word part clues. *The Reading Teacher, 42*, 302–308.

Woodcock, R. W. (2000). *Woodcock Reading Mastery Test-Revised*. Circle Pines, MN: AGS Publishing.

Children's Literature Cited

Ehlert, L. (1993). *Feathers for lunch*. San Diego: Harcourt, Inc.

Lied, K. (1997). *Potato: A tale from the great depression*. Washington, DC: National Geographic Society.

Milne, A. A. (1926). *Winnie the pooh*. New York: E. P. Dutton.

Paulsen, G. (1987). *Hatchet*. New York: MacMillan, Bradbury.

Rathmann, P. (1995). *Officer Buckle and Gloria*. New York: G. P. Putnam.

Seuss, Dr. (1966). *The cat in the hat*. New York: Random House.

Sobol, D. J. (1971). *Encyclopedia Brown tracks them down*. New York: Crowell.

Watkins, R. (1997). *Gladiator*. Boston: Houghton Mifflin.

Wilcox, C. (1993). *Mummies & their mysteries*. Minneapolis: Carolrhoda Books.

Index

A
accuracy, 104-107
Adams, M. J., 112
affixes, 60-61
Allen, J., 99
alphabetic principle, 34, 54-55, 103
alphabet recognition, 53
Anderson, R. C., 69
Angelillo, J., 164
assisted reading, 111-112
authentic, defined, 25
automaticity, 103

B
Baumann, J. F., 99
beanbag toss, 48
Beck, I. L., 89, 99
Betts, E. A., 126
Blachowicz, C., 95, 99
blends, 60
Block, C. C., 99
body language, 178
bulletin boards, 80
Burns, P. C., 127

C
Caldwell, J., 127
Calkins, L. M., 164
comprehension
    activating, developing
        prior knowledge,
        background, vocabulary,
        149-151
    analyzing overall, 136-139
    concepts and, 121
    defined, 119
    difficulties, identifying,
        132-133
    extension activities, 155
    graphic organizers, 154
    interests, motivation, 121
    introducing text, 148-153
    listening level, 131-132
    meaning vocabulary, 120
    modeling at listening
        level, 140-142
    modeling at reading level,
        143
    oral language, 120
    post-reading discussions,
        154
    previewing, 151
    prior knowledge, concepts,
        121, 149-151
    reciprocal teaching,
        155-159
    responding to text,
        153-155

story map, 142
strategies, 122-124, 133-135
struggling with, reasons
    for, 119-124
text factors, 121-122
word recognition, fluency,
    120
comprehension intervention
    framework, 124-139
consonant digraphs, 60-61
content, 18, 20-21, 164-165
context, 34, 84
continuous sounds, 44, 56-57
conventions, 165-169
    legibility, 168-169
    oral, written language, 167
    punctuation, capitalization,
        168
    spelling, decoding problems,
        166
Cooper, J. D., 60, 97, 128
cooperative preview, 152
correct words per minute
    (CWPM) calculation,
    105, 114
Cunningham, A., 52

D
decoding, 21, 34
    word blending, word-list
        reading and, 108-109
    words, 56
DIBELS, 45, 46, 63-64, 70-71
diphthong, 61
discussions, post-reading,
    154

E
Ehri, L. C., 54-56, 103
encoding, 34
extension activities, 155

F
Fisher, P., 95, 99
5-by-5 grid, 68-69
fluency, 101, 120
    See also reading fluency
form, 18-20
framework for core
    instruction, 14-15
    apply, 15
    assess, diagnose, 14
    practice, 15
    reassess, 15
    teach/reteach, 14-15
Fuchs, D., 114
Fuchs, L. S., 114
function, 18, 22

G
Ganske, K., 164
Germann, G., 114
Graham, S., 39
graphic organizers, 154
graphic representations, 84
Graves, D. H., 164
guided preview, 152

H
Hamlett, C. L., 114
Harris, T. L., 102
Hiebert, E. H., 69
high-frequency word lists, 60
Hodges, R. E., 102

I
independent preview,
    152-153
informal reading inventory
    (IRI), 126-127
interactive instruction, 84
Internet resources, keeping
    current and, 197-198
intervention, 13
irregular-word
    recognition, 60
    initial instruction,
        66-67
iteration, 44

J
Johns, J. L., 127-128
journals, periodicals, keeping
    current with, 194-195
journals, writing process
    and, 165

K
Kame'enui, E. J., 99
Kapinus, B. A., 89
keeping current, 191-193
    collaboration with
        colleagues and, 199
    Internet resources for,
        197-198
    journals, periodicals for,
        194-195
    making own plan for, 199
    professional organizations,
        joining, 193-194
    reading professional books
        for, 196
    workshops, classes for,
        196-197
key concept vocabulary,
    83-84
Kiger, N. D., 60, 128
Kucan, L., 99
K-W-L charts, 87

L
LaBerge, D., 103
language components.
    See oral language
    components
Learning First Alliance,
    54–56
Leslie, L., 127
letter combinations, 60-61
letter race activity, 68
letter-sound correspon-
    dences, 63-64, 68, 69-70
letter-sound knowledge,
    initial instruction, 65
letter-sound relationships,
    56-58, 163
listening test administration,
    131-132
list-group-label, 97-98

M
McKeown, M. G., 89, 99
Mangieri, J. N., 99
meaning vocabulary
    acquiring, 78-79
    bulletin boards, 80
    comprehension, 120
    daily discussion of words,
        83
    follow-up activities
        list-group-label, 97-98
        semantic feature
            analysis, 96-97
        synonyms, 95
        word sorts, 98
    increasing, 80-83
    Read Aloud, 82-83
    wide reading, 82
    word banks, word books,
        80
    See also vocabulary
meaning vocabulary inter-
    vention framework, 83-85
modeling oral reading, 108,
    115
Monroe, J. K., 164
morpheme, 19
morphology, 18-19
Morrow, L. M., 129-130
motivation, 12, 121
Muth, K. D., 129-130

O
Oczkus, L. D., 155
onsets, 33
oral language comprehen-
    sion, 120
oral language development,
    17-18
    components, 18-22